Prayer That Works

PRAYER
THAT
WORKS

JILL BRISCOE

MONARCH
BOOKS

First published in the USA by Tyndale House Publishers, Inc.,
Wheaton, Illinois in 2000.
First published in the UK by Monarch Books in 2001.

ISBN 1 85424 512 0

British Library Cataloguing Data
A catalogue record for this book is available
from the British Library.

Designed and produced for the publisher by
Gazelle Creative Productions,
Concorde House, Grenville Place, Mill Hill, London NW7 3SA
Printed and bound in Great Britain by Biddles Ltd
www.biddles.co.uk

To him whom my soul loveth,
who wakens me morning by morning
and helps me rise up with "wings as an eagle".

CONTENTS

THE REASON FOR THIS BOOK

ELMBROOK CHURCH WAS BIRTHED IN PRAYER. FORTY years ago, two families got into their cars and drove around Brookfield, Wisconsin, praying, "Lord, where do you want us to plant a church?" As part of our fortieth-year celebration, my husband (the pastor) called the church to forty consecutive nights of prayer. During this time, he asked me to bring to our congregation eight messages on prayer.

As I prayed about these messages, the Old Testament prophet Elijah came to mind. I had never noticed before how Elijah's story is so often the story of his prayer life. Using incidents in his life, I began an in-depth study about prayer that works. After all, James says of Elijah, "The earnest prayer of a righteous person has great power and wonderful results. Elijah was as human as we are, and yet when he prayed earnestly that no rain would fall, none fell for the next three and a half years! Then he prayed for rain, and down it poured" (James 5:16–18). As a result of my findings about Elijah, I have been greatly challenged in my own spiritual journey. I trust that these pages will do the same for your prayer life as they have for mine.

CHAPTER ONE

PRAYER THAT WORKS

EVER SINCE I WAS A LITTLE GIRL IN WAR-TORN ENGLAND, sitting on a three-legged stool in front of my house waiting for the bombs to fall, I have wanted my prayers to work. I remember praying, "Oh, God, please stop the war." He didn't, and I remember feeling very disappointed with him. Maybe you have prayed that God would stop the conflict raging around you or in your own life, and he hasn't, and you feel disappointed with him too. This book is all about prayer that makes a difference. About prayer that works.

You may wonder what the words *prayer* and *work* are doing in the same sentence. Surely that sounds like an oxymoron! Do you know what an oxymoron is? It's when you put two seemingly contradictory words together, like jumbo shrimp, civil war — or child safe! Prayer and work seem to be opposite concepts. Yet I have discovered that prayer that doesn't work, doesn't work! It takes work to step out of time into eternity — and work to learn the art of leaving things undone so that the greater thing can be done.

Prayer that works isn't merely a matter of personality or gift, although some people have a propensity for praying or have the gift of prayer (and this gift is something that worries the devil very much). Prayer itself is a gracious gift of God in the sense that he made it possible for us to walk right into his presence and talk to him as our Father. Every child of God has that right and privilege.

But if Satan has his way, the first thing to go in our devotional life will be our devotional life! As the little couplet says, "The devil trembles when he sees the weakest saint upon his knees." He will do anything to stop us praying. Sometimes he doesn't have to do anything at all, however, because we assist him by doing away with our prayer life all on our own.

WHEN GOD DOESN'T SEEM TO ANSWER

Often, one of the reasons we stop praying is that we're disappointed with the whole concept of prayer. When we urgently request something from God and he doesn't come through for us, we feel hurt and even betrayed that our prayers have not been answered. That's what happened to me when I was small.

I remember that first urgent attempt to call on the Almighty. The need arose when I became aware that someone was trying to kill me! The Second World War was in full swing, and I had the misfortune to live in Liverpool, a dangerous place. Ships supplying us with food from our allies brought their precious cargo to this seaport, making it a target for the enemy. I was very young, but I was aware that there was a God in heaven, and somewhere deep down in my heart I knew he was perfectly capable of stopping wars and conflicts. I decided one day that I would ask him to stop these terrible airplanes from dropping bombs all over my life.

That night the air raids were particularly vicious. While we were huddled in our underground shelter like little moles, I confidently asked God to intervene. The answer came immediately: The bomb dropped far too near for comfort, damaging the back of our house and sending us running for shelter in the safer environs of the English Lake District. *What went wrong?* I asked myself furiously, trying in my six-year-old mind to make sense out of this nonsense. Had God not heard? Had I said my prayer with the wrong words or in the wrong way? Then came the unwelcome thought: *Perhaps God didn't hear me because he was too busy doing other things, like keeping the stars in place.* And last came the worst thought: *Maybe he couldn't help me because he couldn't help me. He wasn't big enough or strong enough.*

Well, one way or another my fervent request had been ignored, and a huge sense of betrayal gripped me. Somewhere deep down in my six-year-old heart I determined not to try again. Not a few adults have faced similar dilemmas. At the first disappointment they quit without finding out what is happening and what makes prayer work.

If this is the case, the first thing we should do is pray about this. In fact, we should pray about anything that hinders our prayer life. You might want to stop this moment and ask the Lord to identify whatever has caused you to stop talking to him. Then, when you have an inkling of what the blockage has been, talk to him about it.

PRAYER IS PART OF A RELATIONSHIP

Prayer, after all, is the speaking part of our relationship with God. Our relationship with him depends upon our birth, while our fellowship — the quality of our relationship — depends upon our behavior. We must be born of God — "born again" — to be able to talk to God as his children in the first place. After that, our fellowship will be determined by our behavior. Stuart and I have two sons and a daughter. Our blood runs in their veins. Our relationship with them depends upon their birth. If they mess up, our fellowship may be disrupted, but they will always be our children — our estranged children perhaps, but still our children.

Make sure you have been born again. Read the third chapter of John's Gospel and think about it. Pretend you are

Nicodemus. What did Nicodemus need to do after talking with Jesus? What do you need to do after talking with him? Be born again. I've provided a simple outline in the form of an acrostic.

Be still inside. Find a quiet place where you won't be interrupted. Nicodemus came to Jesus "by night" (John 3:2, NKJV). This might have been because he didn't want anyone to see him, but the fact that he came by night also meant that he and Jesus would be alone so they could talk

Open your mind to thoughts from God. The psalmist prayed "Open my eyes that I may see wonderful things in your law" (Ps. 119:18, NIV). Pray, "Lord, Nicodemus came to ask you questions. He had an open mind. Help me to understand what you want from me."

Recognize that God is good — and you are not. Nicodemus was a good man, a clever man, a great teacher of truth. But the best man in the world isn't as good as God wants him to be (see John 3:9–10).

No one is good enough to go to heaven or too bad to be forgiven. Everyone needs to be born again or born from above (see John 3:3–8).

Admit your shortcomings, for "all have sinned and fall short of the glory of God" (Rom. 3:23, NIV). Ask God now to open the eyes of your heart. Ask him to enlighten your mind to understand the good news of the gospel (Eph. 1:18–22; Rom. 3:24). The good news is

- God is good and you are not.
- God loves you and gave Christ to die as your substitute.

- If you believe that Christ died in your place and that God punished him instead of you, you will have eternal life (John 3:16).

Give God your life. Pray, "Here is my life, Lord — all of it. I give you my past — forgive it. I give you my future — secure it. I give you my present — fulfill it."

Accept God's life, eternal life. Pray, "Please come into my life, Lord Jesus, by your Holy Spirit, right now."

Invite him to "fuel and rule" your life from now on. He is the *Lord* Jesus Christ. If he is not Lord of all, he is not Lord at all.

Nourish your new relationship with God. Pray to God and read and apply the Bible every day. "Pray continually, give thanks in all circumstances, for this is God's will for you in Christ Jesus" (1 Thess. 5:17–18, NIV). "Like newborn babies, crave pure spiritual milk, so that by it you may grow up in your salvation, now that you have tasted that the Lord is good" (1 Pet. 2:2–3, NIV).

Once you have established your relationship with God through Jesus Christ, you are ready to work on developing your relationship with him. This is where your devotional life really begins — and prayer is such a large part of that.

MASTER THE ART OF LEAVING THINGS UNDONE
The first thing you need to learn as you begin to pray prayers that work is to master the art of leaving things undone. Many of us suffer from "Martha syndrome". Martha was a woman who loved Jesus very much, but her "much serving" distracted her from focusing on him (Luke

10:40, NKJV). It's hard to leave the urgent thing to attend to one's soul, but the Lord calls us to just such a duty. You have to learn to do it in the middle of the muddle! Martha had good reasons not to sit at Jesus' feet, but those reasons were not enough for the Lord. He said to her, "Martha, Martha, … you are worried and upset about many things, but only one thing is needed. Mary has chosen what is better, and it will not be taken away from her" (Luke 10:41–42, NIV). Many of us can get so excited about the work of the Lord that we forget the Lord of the work, as someone has so aptly said.

Not only do we have to learn the art of leaving things undone, we need to practice the discipline of leaving things uneaten! If we are to work at prayer that works, it may cost us a little belt tightening. Jesus apparently expected us to follow his example in this regard because he said, "when you fast", not "if you fast" (Matt. 6:16). If we are to learn how to step out of time into eternity, there will in all probability be many a breakfast or lunch that will need to go uneaten.

What is more, we may have to leave some hours unslept! Jesus got up a great while before daybreak to meet with his Father (Mark 1:35). It will do us no harm at all to set the alarm clock fifteen minutes earlier each day in order that the most important things are attended to. Sleep deprivation is, after all, better than God deprivation!

SIMPLY GET STARTED

But where do we start when we meet with God? One of the reasons some people avoid personal devotions is a fear of incompetence. *Whatever shall we say when we enter his throne room?* they wonder. Maybe we've always had a problem talking to important people. How do you address the King of kings and Lord of lords? The first thing to do is find a place and time for such an important conversation. Prayer must be planned. There is a sense in which prayer can be engaged in all day long. But time must also be put aside in order to visit with the King, and so plans should be made.

May I suggest that you take your calendar at the start of the week and pencil in time with the Lord every day. To see that appointment there in black and white sometimes helps you to keep it.

Finding a place can be more of a challenge. When I had young children, it was almost impossible to find a quiet spot. In desperation one day, I took the kids out of their playpen and climbed inside! This became a lifesaver for me, and in the busy days after I'd discovered this safe haven, the children learned to leave me alone. They decided that Mommy was a whole lot nicer Mommy when she got out than when she got in!

LEARN TO BE STILL

But I still haven't addressed the problem of what to do when you actually get everything in order and are ready to pray. For instance, what do you do about wandering thoughts?

Let me give you an illustration. We have a cute grand-child, Stephen, who learned at an early age to avoid his mother's eyes when she wanted to talk to him. This necessitated his mom catching up with him and capturing him in her arms. She then turned him around and, taking his little face in a firm grip, got down on his level. Then she said gently, "Look at me, Stephen!" Stephen's eyes rolled to the left, then to the right, then right up to the top of his head until only the whites could be seen! Judy kept at it, holding his little face until, slightly dizzy with all that eye rolling, Stephen finally focused his eyes on his mother's face, and she could tell him what she wanted him to hear. The first thing she said was, "I love you, Stephen." Then she told him what she needed to tell him.

When you begin to pray, imagine that you are Stephen! Think about God, your heavenly Father, taking your face lovingly in his hands and holding you firmly right there in front of him. Imagine him saying to you, "Look at me, Stephen." Stay still until you focus. In other words, be still and know that he is God (Ps. 46:10). When your thoughts are settled on the Lord, you will be ready to pray. It is a good idea to start every time in God's presence with a period of silent prayer.

Try to form a habit of meeting with God without an agenda. So many of us have to teach or care for others that it is hard to come to God without thinking about them. Oh, we think, this Scripture would be excellent for Mrs. Smith. But God has things to say to us as well as to Mrs. Smith. We need to listen to God's voice without thinking of others and what would be good for them. First, God wants to tell us what is good for us. Listening to God is an important part of prayer. Try settling down to spend time quietly. Before you even begin to get down to the work of prayer, see if you can hear a thought, enjoy the stillness, or receive a new idea God wants you to think about.

In Eugene Peterson's paraphrase of the Gospel of Matthew, chapter 6, he gives a contemporary rendering of Jesus' words on the subject:

> Here's what I want you to do: Find a quiet, secluded place so you won't be tempted to role-play before God. Just be there as simply and honestly as you can manage. The focus will shift from you to God, and you will begin to sense his grace. *(The Message)*

In prayer, you have passive parts and active parts. Yet even the passive parts take work for some of us! It takes a huge effort to stop and be still, especially if we are active by nature. In the book of Hebrews, for example, the Lord says, "Make every effort to enter that rest" (Heb. 4:11, NIV). Here Paul puts two words together that do not appear to belong together at all, *effort* and *rest*. That sounds like another oxymoron. I am a very active person. It takes a big effort on my part to be quiet and still, but I must work at resting if I am to have any power in my prayer life. It is only after quieting our spirit that we will know what to pray and how to pray.

LOOK AT THOSE WHO PRAY WELL

There are many ways of learning about prayer. One way is to look at the lives of people who seem to have gotten a handle on it. Who prays prayers that work?

It is said that James, the brother of our Lord Jesus Christ, had a nickname that was given to him by the early church. He was called "camel knees"! The obvious inference is that James's knees resembled those of a camel because he was always kneeling! Hearing this caused me to wonder what my nickname might be!

We're going to take a close look at a prophet named Elijah. James pointed out that "Elijah was a man just like us. He prayed earnestly that it would not rain, and it did not rain on the land for three and a half years. Again he prayed, and the heavens gave rain, and the earth produced its crops" (James 5:17–18, NIV). Now there is a prayer that worked!

What sort of person do you need to be in order to be effective in your prayer life?

First, You Need to Have Been Forgiven by God

Notice that it is the righteous man who has power with God. "The prayer of a righteous man is powerful and effective" (James 5:16, NIV). Another way of looking at that word *righteous* is to realize that it means, among other things, that a person has been forgiven. Are you forgiven?

Years ago I invited a good friend to a meeting. She was not a believer, and she listened carefully to a clear explanation of the gospel. Realizing she was a sinner needing salvation, I introduced her to the speaker at the end of the service. He shook her hand and then said to her, "Tonight you will either sleep as a forgiven sinner or an unforgiven sinner!" She was startled but thought about it and decided to sleep forgiven. Praying a simple prayer of repentance, she asked the Lord Jesus to enter her life, which he graciously did. Now she was ready to pray prayers that were effective.

Second, You Have to Learn to Be Passionate in Your Praying

Elijah "prayed earnestly that it would not rain, and it did not rain" (James 5:17, NIV). Elijah's heart was in his work. Many times we kneel to pray and we really don't care if God hears and answers us or not. Fervency is a condition of the heart that is developed through our growing relationship with God. As we grow to love him, we find ourselves caring about the things he cares about. Prayer turns our thoughts away from our selfish concerns because we are putting ourselves into the presence of a selfless Being — and a little of that rubs off.

Third, You Need to Be a Persistent Pray-er if You Are to See Your Prayers Work

Elijah prayed continually about the work of God. He climbed a mountain and got to work. He set himself to watch and pray until the rain came (1 Kings 18:42–46). Most of us give up far too soon when we are praying. We hit an obstacle such as unanswered prayer and stop dead in our tracks. When Elijah set himself to pray on the top of Mount Carmel, you get the impression that he settled down until the answer came. God likes us to be persistent. Jesus told a story about a woman who persistently asked a judge to grant her request (Luke 18:1–8). And Jesus commended the persistent, blind beggar (Luke 18:35–43). He wants us to go on asking until it's the right time to get an answer.

I think that prayer is a bit like jogging. Years ago I took up running. Everyone in my family was into the sport in a big way, and I didn't want to be left out. They talked enthusiastically about "going through the wall". I wondered what they meant. They explained that if you persisted when you felt you just had to give up, then you went through an invisible wall and got a second wind. It only happened to me once, but I do recall the sense of exultation and the sudden belief that I could run on forever.

I think there is a wall as we engage in prayer as well. It's my belief that when many Christians practice prayer, they live on this side of the wall. They get to what I call the point of push, and they stop instead of pressing on. Next time this happens to you, press on; be persistent and you will find yourself in a new country, a land of joy and freedom, with new hope and expectations. Persistence takes your prayer life into a whole new orbit. "Are any among you suffering? They should keep on praying about it," James tells us (James 5:13).

PRAY WHEN TROUBLE TROUBLES YOU

There should be no excuse for any of us. It's not as if we have nothing to pray about! God has allowed enough trouble in all of our lives to keep us on our knees. And yet for some this could be the sticking point. It's hard to pray when trouble troubles us. Yet James sets his remarks about prayer in the context of trouble. "Is any one of you in trouble? He should pray," he says (James 5:13, NIV). We should, but do we? It has been my experience that my prayer life seizes up as soon as trouble pokes its ugly head into my life. But in the end I look back and recognize that without the trouble there would have been very little praying at all. If we are desperate enough, trouble forces us to spend time with God.

When we first came to live in America, our children were thrilled with the music programs in the public schools. All of them wanted to play an instrument. "I want to play the drums," seven-year-old Pete announced! I was aghast and hastily signed him up for clarinet! This was a serious mistake. The net result of all this was that he never practiced because he didn't want to play the clarinet; he wanted to play the drums. One day he came whistling into the room carrying his clarinet. "Pray for me, Mom," he said. "It's try-outs at school for band, and I want first chair clarinet!"

"I can't pray that for you, Pete. You haven't practiced in months."

"If I'd practiced, I wouldn't need you to pray," he retorted! Many of us are like Pete. We never practice prayer, but when urgent business arises, we expect to know exactly what to say and how to say it. Trouble gives us the grand opportunity to practice for the concert.

What sort of trouble was James talking about? All sorts. Little troubles and big ones. He mentions relational troubles: "Confess your sins to each other" (James 5:16); and he deals with sin troubles: "Whoever turns a sinner from the error of his way will save him from death and cover over a multitude of sins" (v. 20, NIV). Is any among you hurting? Has your spouse left you? Has someone mistreated you at work? Have you been passed over or gotten the bad part of a deal? Is there someone out there friendless, loveless, childless, cash-less, jobless, powerless, clueless? "Is anyone in trouble? He should pray!"

Trouble is a great growth hormone. It takes us from being spiritual dwarfs to spiritual giants — if we respond rightly to it, that is. A few years ago, our family moved into crisis mode. I listened to myself praying. I was shocked. I heard myself praying like an unbeliever. I was praying panic prayers, indulging in angry tirades, and using bargaining language. "Where is my prayer life just when I need it the most?" I asked God. Hard on the heels of that thought came the realization that this trouble was going to do wonders for my prayer life! And it has. Trouble can, in fact, jump-start our prayer life. If we respond to divinely permitted trouble instead of reacting against it, we will find that the situation does two things for us. It will show us that our devotional life isn't working, and it will show us how to work on making it work!

God is such a God of grace. Sometimes he must feel very like the father whose son was in college and who only got in touch when he wanted money! Does the Lord hear from you and me when we want something? The amazing thing about the Lord is his patient love. He will hear us out whenever we get around to approaching him.

So when trouble comes, don't resist it as if it is an enemy; rather, welcome it as a friend. Let it drive you to your knees. Think about it. If trials persist, it just may be that you will persist in prayer. One day I may write a book about the prayers God didn't answer at once. Looking back, I can see how constant pressure kept me in the Lord's presence, and for that I am grateful.

LEARN TO PRAY IN THE DARK

Let's talk about sickness for a moment. James presumes that when we are sick we would want to pray. However, he was probably very aware that it can be difficult to find the energy or the will to turn to God when you are unwell. That's where the church can help. There are some things we should keep in mind when we pray for healing. For one thing, God can heal. He is the source of all health and well-being. The

elders of the church can support the weak person by praying for him or her, especially when the sick one is too sick
to pray. God can heal, there is no doubt about it. But God
may or may not heal. Think of Paul. The apostle had the gift
of healing, yet he himself had a "thorn in the flesh", some
handicap that God did not see fit to heal even though Paul
asked him to. When you can come to the point of saying that
this thorn God has allowed to irritate you — this thorn that
has not been removed — is a good thorn, then you will find
that in acceptance lies peace. At that point, pain can become
the seedbed of prayers that work.

But God is sovereign, and that is the most important
thing. It is also the most sure thing. When God seems to be
taking his time to decide if he will answer our prayers or
not, we should get on our knees and affirm what we know
to be true: God is sovereign, and he truly has everything
under control, despite all seeming evidence to the contrary.
It is hard to believe this if nothing is happening in answer to
prayer. Yet as commentator Matthew Henry says, "God is
sometimes a God who hides himself but never a God who
absents himself, sometimes in the dark but never at a dis-
tance." So you and I need to learn to pray in the dark.
Praying in the dark is soul-building work.

It's difficult to think of God's glory in the dark. But we
must learn to think in this way. God's glory is what real
prayer is all about, after all. We want him to get the glory for
everything in our world, and when he doesn't answer our
prayers at once, we are concerned that his reputation will
suffer. But God is so clever! He is working on so many fronts
all at once. God, unlike us, is other-conscious; he looks
around the situation we find ourselves in and sees all the
players in the drama. He is considering what effect answering our prayer will have on those who are watching. Take
Lazarus, for instance.

Lazarus was sick. He was so sick that his sisters sent for Jesus, who was in a nearby town, to come quickly before their brother died. Jesus, hearing that his friend whom he loved needed him, stayed exactly where he was until he was sure Lazarus was very dead indeed! He told his puzzled disciples that the reason he did this was for the glory of God (John 11:4). Here is a good example of unanswered prayer that would eventually result in the glory of God.

After Jesus finally turned up and raised Lazarus from the dead, he explained that he was doing all this for the sake of the watchers (John 11:42). The watchers were those who would be convinced of Jesus' divinity because of the miracle he would do for Lazarus.

> Meanwhile a large crowd of Jews found out that Jesus was there and came, not only because of him but also to see Lazarus, whom he had raised from the dead. So the chief priests made plans to kill Lazarus as well, for on account of him many of the Jews were going over to Jesus and putting their faith in him (John 12:9–11, NIV).

You see, God is working on many fronts.

Let me illustrate this. When I was a student, I ended up in the hospital. The girl who shared my room was a Christian. One day her pastor came to see her. He prayed that God would heal her. At that time, I was not a Christian, and I was fascinated by what was going on in the bed next to mine. However, God did not see fit to answer that particular prayer that particular day and for good reason. Shortly afterward this girl — who didn't get healed right away — led me to Christ! I was one of the watchers, you see. It really helps to think about this when God appears to be silent. In my case, that girl went through hell so that I could go to heaven. God is superconscious of all the players on the stage of life.

Never be afraid to ask God for the stars, but when God says no or wait, be willing to say, "thy will be done", and ask the Lord for strength to live well in difficult circumstances. As we try to discover the secrets of prayer that works, it is my prayer that we will find our prayer life revolutionized.

∽

A PRAYER ABOUT LOSTNESS

Oh God of love,
who would not that "any" should perish,
but that all would come to Christ and be forgiven:
Hear us now in this quiet moment.
Convince us that your word is true
and that choices are for now,
that there is a heaven where you live
and a hell where you do not.
Jesus said so.

Thank you, Savior,
that we can have you in our hearts
and lives forever.

We pray for our missionaries, pastors, and teachers,
that they would be bold to tell the bad news —
the reality of our lostness —
and then the good news that we can be found,
saved from our sins,
our emptiness, and our wishful wishes.

We pray, too, for our children,
that they believe while young,
grow quickly into Christian maturity,
and serve you till they see you face-to-face!
In Christ's name,
Amen.

Discussion or Journal

These sections can be used by individuals, families, or study groups. If you use this book in a group, then designate a guide leader and follow the outline. If you use the application pages for yourself, then buy a notebook to record your prayers, answers, and discoveries, or use the "notes and ideas" page at the end of each chapter.

1. Can you remember a prayer you prayed that didn't work? What was your reaction?
2. Which of the following phrases caught your attention and why?

   - Prayer that doesn't work doesn't work
   - The art of leaving things undone
   - Learn to pray in the middle of the muddle
   - Sleep deprivation is better than God deprivation
   - Look at me, Stephen
   - Meet with God without an agenda
   - Going through the wall
   - We must learn to pray in the dark

3. Review James 5:13–20. Using the passage, make a list of all the things James says about prayer.
4. Why is it hard to pray when you are in trouble? Why is it hard to praise God when things are going well?

5. Look up John 11:41 and John 12:9–10. How do these two verses relate?

Time to Pray
1. Spend time praying about your prayer life.
2. Tell God about your disappointments in prayer.
3. Pray about the phrase from this lesson that spoke to you.
4. Praise God for the examples of prayers in the Bible.
5. Discuss how hard it is to pray when you are in trouble.
6. Sit in silence until you sense God's grace.

To Do on Your Own
1. Read 1 Kings 18:41–45.
2. Practice praying every day.

Notes and Ideas

CHAPTER TWO
THE HIDDEN LIFE

———————— ❧ ————————

THE OLD TESTAMENT PROPHET ELIJAH WAS A MAN JUST like us. Yet his prayer life probably differed drastically from ours. His prayers worked, whereas our prayer lives need an awful lot of help. When did Elijah learn to have such power in his prayer life? Where did he go to pray? What did he do? Hidden within this man was a vital life of prayer.

BEGINNING AT TISHBE: TIME TO LEARN TO PRAY

> Now Elijah, who was from Tishbe in Gilead, told King Ahab, "As surely as the Lord, the God of Israel, lives the God whom I worship and serve — there will be no dew or rain during the next few years unless I give the word!" (1 Kings 17·1)

The prophet was born at Tishbe. It appears that he had godly parents; they named him after their God. Elijah was one of the many Old Testament names for God, and it meant "creator God". Prayer was no doubt a regular part of Elijah's life when he was growing up. Most people in Tishbe were shepherds, so maybe — like David the psalmist — he learned to pray prayers that worked while in the shepherd's fields.

This gives me encouragement. As a young mom, I struggled with being home with my young children all day. I wanted to be out where the action was. I had been used to

29

being in the midst of all the excitement of youth work. Now, three children later, my worldview had shrunk to the confines of the four walls of our small home, and I felt useless and unimportant.

Then I realized I could use this season of my life to develop my prayer life. I lived in Tishbe! And from there I could travel anywhere in the world. Nothing could stop me from visiting any continent, any country, any town, village, or hamlet on the face of the whole wide world, and I could make a difference for God. All I needed to do was get down on my knees and get to work. After all, Elijah changed the course of history from an obscure corner of the world.

My life changed. I began to thank the Lord for this season of my life. I quit feeling sorry for myself and bought a map. It was during this season that I began to discover the conditions of prayer. I knew that the Bible told us to pray according to the will of God. And I understood that the will of God was revealed in the Word of God. So it was obvious that I needed to get to know God's will through reading the Scriptures. I began to search for and write down the will of God every time I found it in the passage I was reading. I learned that those who had never heard the gospel needed someone to tell them. I read, "How can they hear without someone preaching to them?" (Rom. 10:14, NIV). So I began to pray about that, and as I prayed I started to wonder how I could be the answer to my own prayer.

I believe this is what happened to Elijah. First Kings 17:1 simply says, "Now Elijah, who was from Tishbe in Gilead, told King Ahab, 'As surely as the Lord, the God of Israel, lives — the God whom I worship and serve — there will be no dew or rain during the next few years unless I give the word!'" How did Elijah get from Tishbe to Jezreel, where the king was? While keeping his sheep in Tishbe, I'm sure he prayed about the sinful condition of the nation. And

God showed him how he could be part of the answer: Elijah, himself, could go to Jezreel and speak up where it counted!

As I prayed about the people who didn't know the Lord, I became aware that God was asking me to do something about my situation too.

But what was God asking me to do? Once more I turned to the Bible searching for answers. What could he say to me? As I systematically studied, I came to Philippians 2:7: He "made Himself of no reputation" (NKJV). I knew at once what the Lord was saying to me.

We had been involved with the local youth in the area. Some of them had invited us to visit their local pubs and talk "God" on their own turf. I had declined, fearing someone would see me and misinterpret my motives for going into such places. As I thought about all this, I remembered what I had been reading. Hadn't the Word of God told me that a preacher was God's means of making sure that people heard the gospel? Couldn't I be that preacher? And if Jesus wasn't worried about his reputation, which was what Philippians 2:6–8 indicated, then what was I doing worrying about mine? This was how God showed me his will. From that point on, I began to work among the youth of the area.

The will of God is revealed through the Word of God and confirmed through the Spirit of God. The Holy Spirit is our teacher (John 14:26). If we will allow him to show us what to do in any given circumstance, he promises to take the things of God and clarify them for us. As Elijah began to get the sense that the Lord wanted him to be part of the solution to Israel's dilemma, God undoubtedly confirmed it through his Spirit. The secret of Elijah's public life was his private life. Show me a man or woman who is effective in public, and I'll show you a person who is effective in private. This is the hidden life — that part of a person that develops in apparent obscurity, the part that the Spirit quietly grows up in each of us if we allow it. Because of Elijah's hidden life, he was as effective on his knees as he was on his feet. For Elijah, Tishbe was vital preparation for Jezreel.

I think back on my own life and ministry. And I can now see that my life in Liverpool was my preparation for my life in Lancaster. I think of my life in Lancaster, and I see that it was preparation for my life in Milwaukee. And I think back on my life in Milwaukee and see that this was preparation for my life in the greater environs of the world where I have been privileged to serve. So it is obvious to me that Liverpool — a rather unglorious place where I learned to pray and grow in my hidden life — was a vital part of the whole. Each season of life is important and leads to the next. God's will must be learned each step of the way through the diligent study and application of the Word of God.

So how is this aspect of your hidden life? Are you diligent in searching the Scriptures in order to discern the direction your life must take? Or are you chaffing at life in Tishbe and planning to escape the boredom of small-town living? Why don't you stop right now, lay down this book, and pray about it. God may well leave us in Tishbe until we have learned solitude.

I remember realizing that being isolated in my home with three small children under school age was a Tishbe experience that was planned by God. Once I stopped feeling sorry for myself and began to learn what to do with this forced solitude, I was well on the way to the next stage of my ministry. Tishbe can be a rural home setting, a sickbed, a life of singleness, widowhood, or a period of depression! Tishbe needs to be recognized, and Tishbe needs to be embraced and enjoyed before we are useful in our next location.

From Tishbe to Jezreel: A Time to Speak Up

So I imagine that Elijah found out the heart and will of God while tending his sheep on the wild hills of his hometown. He searched out the will of God for Israel according to the stated purposes of Jehovah. For hadn't the Lord told his people in no uncertain terms that if they served other gods he would register his displeasure by shutting up the heavens until they repented? Some years before, when King Solomon had prayed a prayer of dedication for the temple, he had been mindful of this very thing, saying,

> When the heavens are shut up and there is no rain because your people have sinned against you, and when they pray toward this place and confess your name and turn from their sin because you have afflicted them, then hear from heaven and forgive the sin of your servants, your people Israel. Teach them the right way to live, and send rain on the land you gave your people for an inheritance (1 Kings 8:35–36, NIV).

What made this prayer of Solomon's so significant now, during Elijah's life? Well, this prayer described what the nation was like now under King Ahab.

After King Solomon's death, Jeroboam, the overseer of Solomon's vast public works, had risen to power. Desperate to stay in control, Jeroboam had put a golden calf in two different places of worship because he feared what power the people might have if their worship stayed centralized in Jerusalem. Jeroboam, the son of Nebat "who made Israel to sin", had been bad enough, but his son Ahab was worse. He "did more evil in the eyes of the Lord than any of those before him" (1 Kings 16:30, NIV). He was weak, a compromiser. And he married Jezebel out of political expediency, which was a disaster for Israel.

Jezebel came from Tyre in Sidon, a kingdom in the zenith of its glory. Tyre was queen of the seas, and its colonies dotted the shores of the Mediterranean, reaching as far as Spain and England. When Ahab, the newly crowned consort of Israel, married Jezebel, the match was considered a masterpiece throughout the world. As Jezebel left home, her priests urged her to introduce Ahab to Baal, who was the god of the storms and fertility. Trained under the priests' spells, Jezebel complied.

The worship of Baal involved cruel and hideous rites. Jezebel set about building a temple to her god in Astarta, and she supported 450 prophets of Baal from her own private funds. Then she persuaded Ahab to build a temple with her in Samaria, which was the capitol of the kingdom. This would be like building a temple in London or Washington. The structure was vast, large enough to house immense crowds of people — a megatemple (2 Kings 10:21)!

Soon there were shrines all over the land, and the priests of Baal swaggered about, unhindered, where they would. They were insolent, greedy, debased, and licentious. No wonder it wasn't very long before the fires of persecution began. The prophets of the Lord were hunted and killed. The schools of the prophets were closed. Some think that the verses in Hebrews that speak about those who "wandered about in sheepskins and goatskins, being destitute, afflicted, tormented" (Heb. 11:37, NKJV) refers to this time. A few of God's prophets were saved by Obadiah, who was a secret believer serving in Ahab's court, but the whole land was affected by the apostasy. There were apparently seven thousand secret believers who refused to worship Baal (1 Kings 19:18), but they were paralyzed with fear, and even Elijah was unaware of their existence. All seemed lost, but God was preparing a weak man as his all-sufficient answer. God met with Elijah at Tishbe and sent him to Ahab.

I'm sure that Elijah wondered what he would say to the king when he stood in front of him. The journey to Jezreel was surely spent in prayer. One thing Elijah knew he needed to convey was the fact that the natural disaster God would allow was the direct result of the spiritual disaster Ahab had allowed. Whatever the risk to himself, Elijah had to make sure that both Ahab and his nefarious queen connected the coming years of drought to Baal worship and the country's other sins.

Today the same necessity is laid upon us. We should be voicing the clear warnings of Scripture to everyone who will listen to us. The tendency for people today is to blame God for inflicting them with the consequences of their own choices, when the results are clearly of their own making.

Sexually transmitted diseases are clear examples of people suffering from their own actions. We all know the risks of promiscuity, and we are all responsible for our own actions. I heard about a young businessman who traveled a lot. He was married with a young family, but the road trips got long and lonely. He was a Christian and knew better but one night succumbed to peer pressure and accepted an invitation to go to a party with a woman escort. To his shame he ended up in bed with his companion for the night. The morning dawned, and he realized that he was alone. Feeling terrible about his serious lapse, he got up and walked over to the mirror. To his horror he read the words that had been scrawled on the glass, "Welcome to the world of AIDS!" God allowed the natural disaster that followed to take its course because of the spiritual disaster the young man had allowed. Actions indeed have consequences.

When Elijah finally gained access to Ahab's throne room, we catch the essence of his message to the king: "As the Lord, the God of Israel, lives, whom I serve, there will be neither dew nor rain in the next few years except at my word" (1 Kings 17:1, NIV). The king got the message: That which God allowed was thoroughly connected to that which Ahab had not only allowed but had encouraged. This reminds me of the principle laid out clearly in Romans 1:32: "Although they know God's righteous decree that those who do such things deserve death, they not only continue to do these very things but also approve of those who practice them" (NIV). Elijah may have summed it up this way: "This drought, your Majesty, is the result of your deliberate sin in leading Israel into spiritual adultery." Then Elijah ran down the palace steps and headed for the bushes.

Finding the Courage to Talk to Kings

So where did Elijah find the courage to face Ahab and Jezebel with his ultimatum? Perhaps the clue is found in his words: "As the Lord, the God of Israel, lives, whom I serve" (1 Kings 17:1, NIV). First, he was convinced that he served a living God. The gods of the heathen peoples were no gods at all. Elijah banked everything on the belief that his God lived! And so may we bank everything on the fact that we serve a living God. Other gods are no gods at all compared to our God of gods. Because he lives and we live in him, we can stand before the kings of this world and bring the message of the living Christ to bear on the issues of the day.

It was this sure belief in the living and true God that led me to take a message to a king of my world. My husband and I lived and worked near a large dance hall in a seaside resort. The place drew a huge crowd of music worshipers to its concerts. Concerned for the young people who thronged the place, some of us who worked at a Christian youth center decided to approach the management and see if we could speak to the kids about Christ. I decided to volunteer to be the messenger.

My offer was accepted, and then I began to wonder

what I had done! Standing outside the dance hall, I prayed earnestly for direction. I knew that I was praying according to the will of God as revealed in the Word of God; he had told his disciples to "go into all the world and preach the gospel to every creature" (Mark 16:15, NKJV). I also knew for a fact that only a fraction of the young people in that noisy place would have had the chance to hear the good news that Jesus lived and that he lived to do something wonderful in their lives. But how to deliver my message to the king?

I tentatively entered the "palace" and paid my money. Then I asked to be taken to the manager. A huge bouncer obliged, and I found myself ushered into a dingy little office where the "king" was. Resisting the temptation to address the man as "your majesty", I asked him if I could address the kids from the stage during the intermission.

"Why?" He seemed intrigued by the request. I took a deep breath and, praying hard, told him that the kids needed to know there was a God in heaven who listened to their prayers and who in fact was able to transform their lives. He listened carefully and then granted my request!

Settling down in the man's office, I began answering his many questions about this living God who transforms. I was acutely aware that the living Lord Jesus by his Spirit spoke through me. The God of Elijah is alive and well!

I discovered that standing in the throne room of the real King gives you the nerve to stand in front of the kings of the earth on his behalf. In other words, the hidden life learned in Tishbe, practicing the presence of God, will show itself when God sends you out into public service. As we take on the establishment that is opposed to God, those skills learned in the secret places of the soul will come into their own.

So Elijah drew on his hidden spiritual resources as he spoke to Ahab. He also testified that he was only a servant.

"The Lord, the God of Israel, lives, whom I serve," he said. Elijah counted himself a representative of another. He experienced a sense of sent-ness. This driven need to move out of his comfort zone and speak on behalf of his God took Elijah to places he would never have chosen for himself. He served a higher power than himself and committed himself to do God's will at any cost. A sense of servanthood will do that for us too. Paul spoke of being an ambassador for Christ: "We are therefore Christ's ambassadors, as though God were making his appeal through us" (2 Cor. 5:20, NIV). What a privilege!

This inner necessity to keep your heart in touch with the times is fueled by God in prayer. You cannot pray without bringing yourself in touch with history in the making, because prayer brings you in touch with the one who is making it! Elijah was cognizant of the turmoil, politically and religiously, that existed in Israel. He knew that the old customs and laws were in disarray. Even while he cared for his own sheep, the lost sheep of the house of Israel were heavy on his mind. He mourned the golden days of the reign of Solomon.

As Elijah walked the hot path to Jezreel, I'm sure his heart burned within him. He well knew the effect of drought on cattle and sheep. He realized that his own family would suffer from what was about to happen. But it would be better to die of famine than of a famine of the Word of God, and better to be tortured and killed than for God's name to be maligned and dishonored. Elijah believed that physical suffering was a smaller calamity than moral decay, and he knew that God would not shrink from inflicting such suffering, if that would stop the plague of sin.

You can imagine how Elijah must have felt once his message was delivered and he was safely out of the palace and down the steps. What a relief to be on his way to safety!

He could not have known that his life would be spared when he entered the palace, but no man looks to be a martyr if it's not absolutely necessary, and I can almost hear Elijah's sigh of relief as he ran out of town. But now what? He could hardly return to his home town, as they would be sure to look for him there. He need not have worried. God looks after his own.

LEAVING JEZREEL FOR KERITH:
TIME TO LEARN DEPENDENCE

The voice of God came to Elijah: "Leave here, turn eastward and hide in the Kerith Ravine, east of the Jordan. You will drink from the brook, and I have ordered the ravens to feed you there" (1 Kings 17:3–4, NIV).

"Yes, sure," I would have responded. "I must be hearing voices after my ordeal!" Now remember that we know the rest of the story. God sent the ravens to feed Elijah. Yes, he did. Many of us grew up in Sunday school with that particular picture hanging on the wall. But imagine hearing this for the very first time. Maybe Elijah had no time to quibble with God, as Ahab's soldiers would undoubtedly be searching for him by now. We know that he obeyed God, but we can be fairly certain that Elijah's mind and heart were full of questions.

The man who had begun in Tishbe was now in Kerith. God was making Elijah a man of prayer. Elijah would find out what it was like to have all the props knocked out from under him. Kerith was different from Tishbe in that Elijah was completely alone. No family or neighbors greeted him after a hard day's work. No friends gathered round the campfire at the end of the day to talk about common concerns. Now he was truly alone. All the better to practice listening to God's voice. Now was the time to learn total dependence on God.

Total dependence is almost impossible to learn, of course, unless you are reduced to it. As Mother Teresa said, "You can't say Jesus is all you need until Jesus is all you've got!" But we can recognize the opportunities that come our way to practice "leaning on the Lord" and to allow God to feed us by ravens. What I mean is, let God provide for you in his way. Ole Hallesby says that the basis of all prayer is helplessness. Therefore it should not surprise us to find the props knocked out from under us even as Elijah did. "As far as I can see," said Ole Hallesby, "prayer has been ordained only for the helpless. Prayer and helplessness are inseparable. Only he that is helpless can truly pray." This man believes that God becomes actively engaged at once in hearing and answering the prayer of our helplessness (*Prayer*, 16–17).

If this is true, we should not allow feelings of helplessness to stop us from praying. If helplessness is the real secret of the impelling power of prayer, all of us should take heart! How simple it all is. Prayer consists simply of telling God, day by daily day, how we feel helpless.

Elijah did not have time to prepare for his Kerith experience. It was far too dangerous to stop by the local grocery store on the way out of town and stock up on essentials. But think what he would have lost if he had. He would have missed the ravens. You might think that it wouldn't be a bad thing to miss — depending on birds to care for you! Being fed by ravens is for the birds! But don't miss the point. When we are driven by our naked need to cast ourselves on God, he comes to our rescue in the most unusual ways. So unusual sometimes, we know that God could be the only source of such an answer. Who but God could order ravens to feed us? So helplessness opens a door to the almighty ability of the Lord and thereby assures us of his wisdom and care for us.

Once when I was in the Middle East, a Bedouin shepherd told me what he did when one of his sheep got itself into a difficult situation. "It got itself stuck on a ledge," he said. "The animal was too injured to move much. But I left it alone until it was totally exhausted, because I knew the silly thing would struggle and fall off the ledge. I had to leave it until it was nearly dead before it would let me rescue it." I am ashamed to say that there have been times when I have struggled to get myself out of my own problems. God has left me on the ledge until I, too, have come to the end of my resources, and then he has rescued me.

Only once in my life have I been down to my last bit of cash. We served a mission and pooled our meager funds. One night a young man from our youth group came to tell me he was just ten pounds short of having all his fees for Bible school. A battle began in my heart. Surely God would provide for the young man another way. But the still small voice was insisting I hand over that money. After a long time, I gave him the money. Now I was down to God! I felt an exhilaration I had never experienced before. But good feelings would not buy food. After the young man had gone, I began to panic. I had been irresponsible in giving the money away.

That night my friend from the mission came for a haircut. I loved doing people's hair but was so worried about what I had done that I didn't enjoy her company. I found myself praying helplessly, "Help me, Lord, I'm down to grace." I seemed to hear God say, "This is a very good place to be." When it was time for my friend to go, she shyly handed me an envelope. "I know you never let me pay you," she said, "but please let me do it just this time." I didn't need to open the envelope. I knew what would be inside. Sure enough, God sent the ravens. In that envelope was ten pounds!

When God takes everything away from you, remember

Kerith and realize that your outside circumstances can be an opportunity to depend completely on God. Kerith could be a serious illness, where you find yourself isolated for an unknown period of time. Once, when I found myself in such a position, a friend sent me a little poem.

> *The world says laid aside by illness,*
> *but Christ says, called aside for stillness.*

This was my opportunity to practice dependence. Kerith can be loneliness. Perhaps your husband is out of town — or maybe you don't have a husband! One way or another, you have little companionship at the moment. Make the most of this period of time to savor being "down to God". Kerith may be financial ruin or divorce, a career move or old age. Whatever Kerith is for you, try to recognize what God is allowing to happen, and thank him that you are down to grace. Remember that when you are down to grace, you are down to God. Then watch out for the ravens!

❧

A PRAYER TO PRAY IN TISHBE

> *Lord, this is Sunday,*
> *the day the Puritans called the market day of the soul.*
> *Help us to do business with you — before the day is*
>   *through.*
>
> *You are the Father of lights.*
> *Show us your faithfulness in your world,*
> *in your Word, and in your Son — before the day is through.*
>
> *We pray for those in trouble,*

for those planning suicide,
for those who have grown weary
fighting for their marriages.
Use your children, Lord, to intervene,
to bring faith and love into their lives —
before the day is through.

And God, we pray for little children,
those who represent the best of your thoughts.
Help them know that God can meet them in their
  nightmares
and wake them up to his comfort, presence, and power —
before the day is through.

And particularly, Lord,
we pray for our missionaries and the people they care for.
May each be conscious that today he or she is a walking
statement of your image here on earth —
before the day is through.

There are problems, Lord — help us solve them.
There are heartaches, Lord   help us heal them.
There are material needs — instruct us how to meet
  them —
before the day is through.

God, forgive us, have mercy on us all! Meet us now.
Do business with us in this holy market place —
before the day is through.
Amen.

Discussion or Journal

1. Review 1 Kings 17:1–6.
2. Spend time in silent reflection on the material.

3. What does Tishbe represent to you?
4. Have you ever "lived at Tishbe"? What lessons did you learn about prayer?
5. How has your life at Tishbe been preparation for your life now?
6. List three things you have learned about the will of God from this lesson.
7. List five things you have learned about Ahab and Jezebel.
8. What does Kerith represent?
9. How do you respond to the concept "helplessness is the basis for prayer"?
10. What does it mean to be "down to grace"?

Time to Pray
1. Thank God for the Tishbes and Keriths of your life.
2. Pray about the will of God for your world.
3. Pray for those who are serving the living and true God at home and abroad.
4. Pray for yourself.

To Do on Your Own
1. Read 1 Kings 17:1–24.
2. Search the Scriptures to discover the will of God for the world and for your life.
3. Accept — and even embrace — your helplessness.
4. Watch for the ravens, God's provisions for your life.

Notes and Ideas

CHAPTER THREE

LIVING IN A HOT SPOT

━━━━━━━━━━━━━━━ ⚭ ━━━━━━━━━━━━━━━

WHEN WE LEFT ELIJAH AT THE END OF CHAPTER 2, HE was being cared for by ravens sent by God. I can imagine that, once Elijah saw that God would indeed take care of him, he sort of settled into this odd but comfortable existence. We see, though, that life at Kerith didn't stay comfortable.

> But after a while the brook dried up, for there was no rainfall anywhere in the land. Then the Lord said to Elijah, "Go and live in the village of Zarephath, near the city of Sidon. There is a widow there who will feed you. I have given her my instructions." (1 Kings 17:7–9)

I wonder if Elijah would ever have moved on if God hadn't allowed the river to dry up? The prophet must have been a little surprised when the stream was reduced to a trickle and the ravens didn't bring his breakfast one morning. God can move and guide us through circumstances or nature as he wills, and he wanted to make sure that his messenger got the message.

LOOK FOR GOD'S HAND IN THE CIRCUMSTANCES

We need to look for the hand of God in the things that happen to us. Perhaps you have lost your job through no fault of your own, and the source of supply — namely, your income — has dried up. The ravens have stopped delivering the goods, and you are forced to move on. Trust God to look after you.

Elijah had no idea how long the drought would last. If he had known the future, perhaps he would have been reticent to move out of his comfort zone and obey God. He may also have wondered if he had heard God correctly. Had the still small voice really said, "Go to Zarephath"? Surely not. After all, Zarephath was Jezebel's hometown! It was there that the priests of Baal had schooled the young princess in her religion. Was the Lord really sending Elijah to the very town that appeared to be the scariest and most dangerous place? Yes, Elijah must have wondered if he had misheard the Lord. So perhaps God, knowing his servant's misgivings, made sure Elijah moved on by allowing the source of supply to dry up. He knew that the very safest place in his part of the world was the one place that Jezebel would never think of looking for him! And so it turned out to be.

Elijah probably traveled by night, and I can imagine him puzzling over the strange instructions of the Lord. What did it all mean? What widow would meet him, and how would she be able to help him and possibly hide him from the authorities? And why would God choose a woman from another culture to take care of him rather than a woman in Israel? Perhaps the answer to that was that God looks on the heart. He, who sees the inner recesses of our hearts and minds, knows who will respond to him if they only have the chance.

LOOK AT PEOPLE AND SEE WHAT GOD SEES

Remember how clever God is. He works on so many fronts at the same time. Yes, he needed to hide his servant from Ahab and Jezebel, but he wanted to bring his message of truth to a poor lost woman who didn't have the knowledge that the widows of Israel had. This way, God could accomplish his purposes for both Elijah and the widow. It's easy to judge by appearances, isn't it? We all do it. God doesn't, however.

Remember Samuel's mistake when he was told to go to David's hometown and anoint a new king (1 Sam. 16)? When Samuel arrived, he didn't know whom God would have him appoint. As Samuel sat at the feast given in his honor by David's father, his heart leapt with joy and admiration when he saw Jesse's eldest son. Surely Eliab was the Lord's anointed. Eliab was such a fine figure of a man. He was tall, good-looking, and Jesse's eldest, having obvious status in the family. But what impresses us doesn't always impress the Lord. In this case, a young shepherd boy left out of the party to care for the sheep was the man after God's own heart and his chosen one. In essence, God said to Samuel, "Don't look on his height, look on his heart."

> But the Lord said to Samuel, "Do not consider his appearance or his height, for I have rejected him. The Lord does not look at the things man looks at. Man looks at the outward appearance, but the Lord looks at the heart" (1 Sam. 16:7, NIV).

How often do we look at the outside? Image is everything in our culture, and only God can help us see what he sees and choose what he chooses.

Who, meeting the impoverished widow that day at Zarephath, would have believed she had been spoken to by God? Yet the Bible says the Lord had commanded her to feed him (1 Kings 17:9). We are not told how he had so commanded her, but there is no doubt she was prepared. As soon as the unkempt figure of Elijah appeared and asked her to share her last meal with him, she complied without any argument (1 Kings 17:15).

There have been many times in my own life when I have looked at people — without having brought them to God in prayer — and made judgments that have proved to be wrong. This was especially true when I was engaged in youth work. The appearance of some of the wild young men and women was such that we could have been forgiven for not expecting them to be interested in the gospel. Yet the wildest and the woolliest were often the ones who were the first to ask the most piercing questions — and the most eager to commit themselves to Christ once their questions had been satisfactorily answered. I learned to pray hard and ask the Lord what he saw, instead of leaning on my own understanding. Now I try not to "look on their height, but rather to look on their hearts".

TAKE ONE STEP AT A TIME

Elijah realized that Zarephath was not a resort center. the name Zarephath means "smelting furnace". That wouldn't be an encouraging thought! What sort of hot spot would it be? Elijah would soon find out.

Elijah would learn to pray as diligently as he had prayed in Kerith, and God would hear and answer his daily request for bread. The Lord made sure that Elijah was dependent enough on him to stay close, so that he would be able to hear God's voice.

So he went to Zarephath. As he arrived at the gates of the village, he saw a widow gathering sticks, and he asked her, "Would you please bring me a cup of water?" As she was going to get it, he called to her, "Bring me a bite of bread, too."

But she said, "I swear by the Lord your God that I

don't have a single piece of bread in the house. And I have only a handful of flour left in the jar and a little cooking oil in the bottom of the jug. I was just gathering a few sticks to cook this last meal, and then my son and I will die."

But Elijah said to her, "Don't be afraid! Go ahead and cook that 'last meal', but bake me a little loaf of bread first. Afterward there will still be enough food for you and your son. For this is what the Lord, the God of Israel, says: 'There will always be plenty of flour and oil left in your containers until the time when the Lord sends rain and the crops grow again!'"

So she did as Elijah said, and she and Elijah and her son continued to eat from her supply of flour and oil for many days.

For no matter how much they used, there was always enough left in the containers, just as the Lord had promised through Elijah (1 Kings 17:10–16).

Having to ask a starving person to share her last meal with him must not have come easily for Elijah. It would not come easily for any of us! But Elijah was looking for confirmation of the message God had given him. God had said that he had given a widow instructions to feed him. But he had not said which widow. God never gives us all the information at once. Our way is made clear step-by-step and little by little. We must practice daily dependence.

I remember Stuart and I becoming convinced that we were to leave the business world and go into full-time Christian service. The conviction was born in us that this was the Lord's will. At that point, we had no idea what we should do and where we should do it. If we had known that the decision would lead to months of separation from one another, we may not have moved from Kerith on to

Zarephath! But God in his grace veils the future from us and says, "Trust me; do what you know to do in the here and now, and I will look after the future." I have learned that God is waiting around the corner of tomorrow, with my future in his hands, and my job is to be responsive to what I know of his will today. This way, you find yourself praying all the time, which is a nice result of uncertainty.

I can imagine Elijah saying to the Lord, "Well here's a woman, but she looks as though she's on her last legs. Surely she can't be the one to look after me." And I can imagine the Lord suggesting that Elijah ask her for her last meal, to find out! When she complied, Elijah knew she was the one. Step-by-step and little by little.

What guidance are you seeking? Are you busy doing what you know to do this moment and this day? Or are you expecting God to present you with the blueprint before you build your life? Thank God right now for the things that are clear to you, and tell him that you'll trust him for the rest.

DO THE BORING WORK

Elijah settled down in Zarephath to wait out the drought. The Lord made sure there was enough oil and bread each day, and somehow the days passed. It must have been strange to live with an unbelieving family after being surrounded by Jehovah worshipers in his own home in Tishbe. Among other things that Elijah settled down to learn was what it took to pray for a family that didn't know the one true God.

Do you live in such a family? How many of us live with beloved unbelievers and struggle to know how to pray prayers that work for them? Many of us have a problem because we are too close to the situation. It's hard to pray rationally when you love people so much and you are desperately concerned about their spiritual well-being. Maybe you have done your level best to lead them to Christ over the years, and everything you have said has fallen on deaf (or worse, indifferent) ears. You may even have given up talking about it at all.

Rick Warren, pastor of Saddleback Church in Lake Forest, California, is quoted as saying, "People may resist our advice, spurn our appeals, reject our suggestions, and not accept our help, but they are helpless against our prayers." I believe that with all my heart. God took Elijah from a safe spiritual environment, put him in the middle of what was very likely a Baal-worshiping family, and said, "Let's see what this hot spot will do not only for your relationship with me but your relationship with this family. Undoubtedly it will do great things for your prayer life for unbelievers!" God wanted Elijah to know that he possessed a secret weapon, the secret weapon of prayer. Prayer is our secret weapon in these situations. Remember what James said about fervent prayer: He said it was dynamic in its working. Prayer is in fact, dynamite. In his book, *Prayer*, Ole Hallesby says, "The work of the Spirit can be compared to mining. The Spirit's work is to blast to pieces the sinner's hardness of heart and frivolous opposition to God. The period of the wakening can be likened to the time when the blasts are fired to the time when the deep holes are being bored with great effort into the hard rock. To bore these holes is hard and difficult and a task which tries one's patience." (77).

This is a pretty graphic picture. The idea of prayer boring holes into hard hearts so the dynamite of the Spirit can be buried there helps me realize two things. First, my job is to do the boring. Second, it's God's job to blast away the hardness of people's hearts. The problem is that it's boring to do the boring! But it must be done.

I imagine that, day after boring day, Elijah did the work of prayer, having faith that as he did his part, God would do his. He may have prayed that the widow's eyes would be open to the truth he sought to teach and that the evidence of God's provision would convince her that Elijah was truly the servant of the highest God. And I'm sure that what he prayed for the widow he also prayed for her son. Mining can be tiring, but the results can be spectacular. Before long, Elijah would learn never to underestimate what the Holy Spirit had been doing before he arrived on the scene. This reminds me of a story in the New Testament:

Cornelius was a God-fearing man but a Gentile who didn't know Christ. God, looking at Cornelius's heart and not his height, sent the apostle Peter to him to explain how he could come to faith. Peter, being a "true-blue Jew", didn't want to go to the house of a Gentile. However, God told him to go anyway, and when Peter arrived and heard the man's story, he was amazed and said, "I now realize how true it is that God does not show favoritism but accepts men from every nation who fear him and do what is right" (Acts 10:34–35, NIV). The Holy Spirit had been at work preparing Cornelius for Peter and Peter for Cornelius. God surely hears the cry of the seeking soul.

Once I was driving to a youth center in the English countryside. It was in the days when it was safe to hitchhike, and the youth of Europe were on the move. I stopped to pick up three German young people and never dreamed this was a special part of God's plan for all of us. I had prayed that morning that God would use me to help someone, but I never expected that he had already heard and answered that prayer. As I talked with my passengers, they told me they were all theology students. I was delighted, thinking we would share some good fellowship. However, the girl sitting beside me, who seemed to be the spokesperson for the three, said, "We are seeking God!"

I nearly drove off the road. "What do you mean?" I asked.

"We all entered theology college in order to find out if indeed there was a God at all. We have not found him yet." My heart began to race. Before I could say anything, another girl explained, "We came on this trip in order to make one last search for him. We agreed that if we didn't find anyone to help us we would give up the search and drop out of school." Then she added, "But I don't know why I'm telling you all this."

"I do," I said. So I took them along to the Christian center, where the leader spoke fluent German, and he led them all to Christ! When God looks into the hearts of men and women and sees a heart looking for him, he makes sure one of his servants is sent to help them find him.

This should cause us to get up each and every morning of our lives and go out into our day with a huge sense of expectation. We can be assured that someone, somewhere has been "mining" and that the Holy Spirit has been at work in the circumstances in order to bring the seeking soul and the servant of the Lord together. How can life be anything but exhilarating for the disciple of Jesus! So in this matter of prayer, we must never discount what the Holy Spirit has been doing before we arrive on the scene.

REMEMBER JESUS' PRAYERS FOR US

We must never discount the prayer ministry of Jesus Christ. Once we realize that the Godhead — God the Father, God the Son, and God the Holy Spirit — is involved in the prayer life of the believer, a new confidence is born in our hearts. "Why," our spirit says when a sudden opportunity or word of wisdom visits us, "this is God's idea, not mine!" The ministry of our great High Priest is shown in the book of Hebrews 5:4–7.

Therefore, since we have a great high priest who has gone through the heavens, Jesus the Son of God, let us hold firmly to the faith we profess. For we do not have a high priest who is unable to sympathize with our weaknesses, but we have one who has been tempted in every way, just as we are — yet was without sin. Let us then approach the throne of grace with confidence, so that we may receive mercy and find grace to help us in our time of need (Heb. 4:14–16, NIV).

This passage not only talks about us feeling confidence in approaching a holy God with our requests, it also speaks of the fact that Jesus is praying for us even as we pray for others! What an incredible thought! Stop right now and tell yourself, "Jesus is praying for me."

This was brought home to me in the most dramatic fashion one day, at a low point in my life. Lying in bed one morning, I willed myself to get up and face the day. As I readied myself, I found my spirits lifting. By the time I had eaten breakfast, my soul was tap dancing. Standing quite still in the kitchen, I said to myself, *Someone must be praying for me.* Immediately God's quiet whisper spoke in my mind: *I am.* I stopped in my tracks, savoring the moment. Jesus was praying for me — no wonder my spirits were soaring!

Not only does Jesus pray for us, but he prays with us. He is infinitely concerned about those we love and for whom we pray, and he wants to pray with us for them. Hallesby writes:

You will see wonderful things in your prayer room. You will see your eternal High Priest on his knees in prayer. You will see him beckon to you and ask you to kneel beside him, and you will hear him say, "You love these dear ones of yours, but I love them even more. I have created them. I have died for their sins. I have followed them all the way. You and I both love them, now let us both pray them into the kingdom of heaven. Only do not be weary and discouraged if it takes time" (*Prayer*, 54).

What are you discounting as you pray? The work of the Holy Spirit or the prayer work of Jesus Christ? You are not alone in this battle of prayer. God is for us, and "if God is for us, who can be against us?" (Rom. 8:31, NIV). So count on the Trinity, and get to work.

LEARN TO ASK BUT NOT INSTRUCT

Finally, as you get to work praying when you're in a hot spot, learn to ask but not instruct. Remember that God already knows what he will do to answer your prayers. Hallesby says:

> We think we should help God answer our prayers. We think we should suggest how he should go about giving us the answer. Even though we do not give expression to it, we think like this. "Dear God, this is what I am earnestly asking of thee. I know that it is difficult, but if thou wilt do so and so, thou canst accomplish it" (*Prayer*, 47).

We make use of prayer for the purpose of commanding God to do our bidding. We need to stop asking for printouts or progress reports.

I think of Jesus' testing his disciples in the Gospel accounts. After teaching the multitudes and healing the sick, he told the disciples to feed the people. "Where shall we buy bread for these people to eat?" he asked Philip (John 6:5, NIV). Then the Scripture says, "He asked this only to test

him, for he already had in mind what he was going to do"
(v. 6, NIV). Philip failed the test, for he didn't relate the need
to the Christ who could meet it. He didn't say, "Lord, feed
the multitude and do it your way. Show me how to be a part
of the answer." Instead he left Christ out of the reckoning
and set about forming a committee and working on a bud-
get (v. 7)! Philip looked at a multitude of need and gave up.

In *The Message*, Eugene Peterson renders Jesus' words in
Mark 11:23: "Embrace this God-life. Really embrace it, and
nothing will be too much for you. This mountain, for
instance: Just say, 'Go jump in the lake'... and it's as good as
done." This "God-life", as Peterson calls it, is the life of faith.
It works on the basis of trust and obedience, and its lifeblood
is prayer. Its basis is helplessness, and its chief word is *ask*.
"Ask. Just ask me," says Jesus, "and see what I will do for you.
Ask me, and don't tell me how."

> *Ask me to do it but don't tell me "how."*
> *Ask him to answer but don't tell him now.*
> *Ask him to give you the strength for the task,*
> *Then thank him for giving much more than you ask.*
> *Ask him to cleanse you whenever you pray,*
> *Be honest with God at the end of the day.*
> *Ask for the power and faith it will take,*
> *To say to this mountain, "Go jump in the lake!"*

Elijah in the school of prayer learned to "ask". God gave him
hot spots to live in, to bring him to dependence so that he
could practice exercising faith. He could well have asked
God to feed him and then suggested that God show him
where the prophets Jezebel was persecuting were hiding so
that he could join them. But he left it up to God, trusting
him to take care of matters in his way. And God came
through, which he always will. It's so much more exciting

this way. So we "ask him to do it but don't tell him how". Then "we ask him to answer but don't tell him now".

When you're praying for your family, it's so easy to grow impatient. What if something happens to them before they find the Lord? Maybe someone is sick, and it seems obvious to you that God has to intervene now. But God's clocks keep perfect time. "God time" is not to be confused with "people time".

Think about old Zechariah. One day when he was very old, he was in the Temple praying for the people (Luke 1:8–9). Suddenly an angel appeared and said, "Do not be afraid, Zechariah; your prayer has been heard" (Luke 1:13, NIV). For a moment I can see the old man casting around in his mind, desperately trying to make sense out of it. Which prayer? The one he had just prayed for Israel? Then the angel made it clear. "Your wife Elizabeth will bear you a son" (v. 13, NIV). Oh, *that* prayer! I can imagine Zechariah secretly thinking, *Your timing is awful, Lord.* But God's clocks keep perfect time, and John was born in the fullness of time and for the purposes of God.

We need to realize that none of our prayers fall to the ground. I believe that every prayer we ever pray hangs, as it were, in space, until God answers it according to his eternal purposes. We may not see it answered, or like the old priest, we may be very old before we do, but we can have faith that one day our mountain will "go jump in the lake". I have been learning to watch for the answers to my "old" prayers, rather than demand answers to my "new" ones.

One day our eldest son walked in a deep valley of sorrow. It was a bitter place to be. He serves on the staff of our church, and there was much support for him and many prayers. As parents of an adult child, all Stuart and I could do was watch and pray. It's a difficult thing to bear private grief publicly, but David bore his grief with dignity and grace.

One day as we were sharing our hearts together, I was reminded of a little boy kneeling by the side of his bed saying his prayers. He was six years of age at the time, and I remember stopping as I passed his door and being struck with the picture. I also remembered what I prayed in that moment of time. I prayed, not realizing the significance of my words, "Lord, make this child a man of dignity and integrity." Then I added, "whatever it takes."

That day as we talked, I recognized the answer to my "old" prayer. It had taken sorrow to answer my prayer, but it had been answered, and I murmured under my breath, "Oh, I see, Lord, this is that answer," and I worshiped.

One of my favorite hymns says:

Praise to the Lord, who o'er all things so wondrously reigneth,
Shelters thee under His wings, yea, so gently sustaineth!
Hast thou not seen, how thy desires e'er have been
Granted in what He ordaineth?

It's hard to pray for one of your loved ones that starts with "Whatever it takes, Lord," but if you can manage it, God will handle it tenderly for you and help you to handle it too. So when God answers a past prayer in the present, praise him for it however hard it is, and one day he will answer your present prayers in your future, you'll see.

Our prayers "in a hot spot" do count. What also counts is the kind of people we become while we're residing in Zarephath.

A Prayer about a Hot Spot

Am I like a tea bag
waiting to know,
what flavor I am
when in hot H_2O?

Am I like a tea bag
soggy and wet?
Am I asking the Lord
just how hot it can get?

I want to be able
to give out for sure
a fragrant aroma
that makes folks want more.

But that means hot water
that hurts my deep pride,
that cleans out my life
till I'm tired inside,
of a fragrance-less life
that knows not how to sing —
So dip me in water,
but keep hold of the string!
Amen.

Discussion or Journal

1. Read the account of Elijah's time with the widow, in 1 Kings 17:7–16.
2. Why wouldn't Elijah want to go to Zarephath?
3. Has God ever let the "river" dry up so you had to move out of your comfort zone? What did you learn?

4. Have you ever judged someone by appearances? What does this story teach you? See also 2 Corinthians 5:12.

5. Do you find it hard to pray for people who don't know Christ, especially those near to you? Discuss the concept of "mining" as Hallesby related the image of "boring" to prayer.

6. Read the story of Cornelius in Acts 10. What do you learn about prayer from Peter and Cornelius?

7. Do you know that Jesus Christ never stops praying for you? Write down three things you learned about the high priesthood of Christ. See also: Hebrews 4:14–15; 5:5; and 7:25.

8. Review the poem "Ask me to do it" on page 56. Discuss the first two lines. What does the story in Luke 1 add?

Time to Pray
1. Praise God for the hot spots in your life and what you've learned of him.

2. Pray for all the unlikely people in your life who don't appear to be interested in Christ.

3. Practice praying "ask" prayers without telling God how to answer them!

4. Make a list of widows God has put in your life. Promise God you will pray for them.

5. Pray about your prayer life.

To Do On Your Own
Read 1 Kings 17:17–24.

Notes and Ideas

CHAPTER FOUR

THE UPPER ROOM

————————— ❧ —————————

AHAB SEARCHED THE KNOWN WORLD FOR HIS ENEMY Elijah. As Obadiah, Ahab's right-hand man, told Elijah much later, "There is not a nation or kingdom where my master has not sent someone to look for you" (1 Kings 18:10, NIV). Everywhere but Zarephath. Hidden in the one place the king never dreamed of looking, Elijah and the widow and her son stayed safe.

How do you pass the time of day when there is nothing to do? I imagine that Elijah spent a fair bit of it in prayer.

I have learned to try and use downtime for the Lord. Since I travel so much, it's tempting to get to my hotel room, kick off my shoes, and turn on the TV. Or, finding a surprise hour of space after work, my hand automatically reaches for a magazine. Living with unbelievers can make it difficult to make time for God. You don't want to always be disappearing to have your devotions. It looks a bit pious or "holier than thou". Yet if we don't take advantage of the unexpected, still periods of our lives, we may be caught off guard when trouble comes.

PREPARING FOR TROUBLE

When Jesus was in Gethsemane, he asked the disciples to watch and pray with him, but the disciples fell asleep. Twice the Lord woke them up. "Watch and pray so that you will not fall into temptation. The spirit is willing but the body is weak," he said (Matt. 26:41, NIV). When the crucial time came, with Judas leading the temple guard to arrest Jesus, the disciples ran away (v. 56).

When the body is weak, the spirit may be willing, but not for long! You never know when there is a difficult task waiting for you around the corner of tomorrow. Jesus gave no indication that the disciples' weariness excused them from prayer. He, knowing what was ahead, knew what the results of their lack of discipline would be. But what do you do with tired bodies and wandering thoughts? All of us struggle with this one.

One thing I do is to pray about it. Praying about your praying is a great idea! Just tell the Lord that you can't concentrate or you're really tired, and ask him to keep you awake. Then you can corral wandering thoughts by praying about them. When a renegade thought intrudes into my mind — and it happens all the time — I sometimes hold it by the throat, as it were, and stop and talk to the Lord about it. The thing to do is recognize the prayer problem at once, stop and deal with it, and then continue.

It helps sometimes to read a verse of Scripture first; that helps me focus. But if all else fails, I allow myself to think about the distraction and in fact pray about it. Sometimes a distraction is like a demanding child. Nothing else can get done until you attend to its demands.

Some time later, the woman's son became sick. He grew worse and worse, and finally he died. She then said to Elijah, "O man of God, what have you done to me? Have you come here to punish my sins by killing my son?"

But Elijah replied, "Give me your son." And he took the boy's body from her, carried him up to the upper room, where he lived, and laid the body on his bed. Then Elijah cried out to the Lord, "O Lord my God, why have you brought tragedy on this widow who has opened her home to me, causing her son to die?" (1 Kings 17:17–20).

Elijah was ready when trouble came calling at the widow's house, which makes me think he had been using his time well.

We don't know how long the widow's family lived in peace before trouble came. But trouble did come in the shape of a lingering sickness. The little boy fell ill. I can imagine the worried widow making trips to the temple. I can hear her urgent prayers. I can also see the man of God on his knees, urgently pleading for healing. Now, God can heal, but he doesn't always heal. If I had been in Elijah's shoes, I would have considered this request a "must" for an answer in the affirmative! After all, hadn't Elijah been telling the widow that God was the God of gods? Can you imagine the consternation when, despite all their pleading, the boy "finally" passed away? The word *finally* denotes "after a long time". There is no greater nightmare than to watch a beloved child slowly die.

Once all hope was gone however, the widow gathered her son in her arms and burst out at Elijah, "O man of God, what have you done to me? Have you come here to punish my sins by killing my son?" (1 Kings 17:18). What did she mean?

Like many people, she thought God was punishing her for some sin she had committed. In most early religions, people thought of gods as entities that were easily angered by human behavior. It's easy to think like that even as a believer in Christ. The wages of sin, however, is death, not suffering. If you and I were punished for our sins, we would all be crucified tomorrow! In this case, one reason God allowed the little boy to die was in order to bring spiritual life to the whole family.

Elijah certainly had questions of his own. "Give me your son," he said to the widow. Taking the child's body from her arms, he carried him to his upper room and laid him on his bed (v. 19). Then he asked God, "O Lord my God, why have you brought tragedy on this widow who had opened her home to me, causing her son to die?" (v. 20).

Bringing Our Whys to God

Prayer is a place where we can ask all our whys. We must not demand that our whys be answered, but we can ask them out loud and know that God feels our pain. The Bible tells us that God enters into the agony of his people. "In all their suffering he also suffered, and he personally rescued them" (Isa. 63:9). He wants to tell us what he knows we can bear. I only know that when I bring my whys to him in worship, I leave the throne room without them. Ruth Bell Graham captures this perfectly in her poem "Sitting by My Laughing Fire":

> *I lay my whys*
> *Before Your cross*
> *In worship kneeling,*
> *My mind too numb*
> *For thought,*
> *My heart beyond all feeling.*
> *And worshiping,*
> *realize that I*
> *In knowing you*
> *don't need a "why".*

Ruth is talking about the ability to let go of something that's very painful. Tough things mustn't stop our prayers; they must drive us to prayer.

Notice that Elijah's why didn't keep him from praying; in fact, it appears to have driven him to more fervent petition. "And he stretched himself out over the child three times and cried out to the Lord, 'O Lord my God, please let this child's life return to him'" (1 Kings 17:21). That was pretty bold. And in this instance God answered his prayer.

> The Lord heard Elijah's cry, and the boy's life returned to him, and he lived. Elijah picked up the child and carried him down from the room into the house. He gave him to his mother and said, "Look, your son is alive!"
>
> Then the woman said to Elijah, "Now I know that you are a man of God, and that the word of the Lord from your mouth is the truth" (1 Kings 17:22–24, NIV).

Can you imagine their joy? I find it hard to grasp what went on in the little house that evening, as Elijah, the widow, and her son talked. Not only had God given life, but he had also given light. The word from Elijah's mouth was true! His God was God indeed, and the widow and her son acknowledged it.

I can imagine that this incident in the prophet's life would stand him in good stead when the test came later, as we shall see, on Mount Carmel. If God could raise a dead child, he could send down fire from heaven. But then, all answered prayer should build our confidence. Look back and think of a prayer that worked, of a God who was faithful to you. God is the "same yesterday, today, and forever" (Heb. 13:8). Let yesterday's answers give you hope for today's dilemmas. And remember, as the saying goes, "You are coming to a king, large petitions with you bring."

WATCHING FOR ANOTHER'S CHILD

Look at this picture. Elijah stretches out his arms to the grieving mother and says, "Give me your child." That's what we can do for each other. Do you know any mothers with children in trouble? I do. Have you ever stretched out your arms and said to that frantic one, "Give me your child"? Then have you carried the child to the upper room of prayer and laid him or her before the Lord? Have you pled for life to come into the deadness, health to replace the sickness, and a new chance at life? Sometimes a mother is beyond the ability to pray these sorts of things anymore; these are times when we can pray for her. Once I had an experience like this, but I was on the receiving end.

It was a long time ago, when my children were all teenagers. The dating years were upon us, and I lived in a permanent state of internal panic. Fortunately I had a husband who reveled in those years, and so I leaned on him. One day, however, he was away, so I couldn't "lean", and a young man asked my young daughter, Judy, to the school dance. I panicked, until she explained I could come and chaperone. At that I gladly gave permission and the invitation was accepted. Then I looked in my appointment book. Both my husband and I had meetings out of town on the day of the dance. Neither of us could chaperone! I panicked. Suddenly this perfectly nice young man took on another image in my imagination.

I couldn't get out of my commitment, and so I arrived at the meeting in total spiritual disarray. Looking at the program, I saw that there was a prayer room. I made a beeline for it and met Margaret, whose ministry it was to help people like me!

I explained my problem, and she listened to me patiently and gave me some Scripture. Then she said I would need to let my daughter go. "After all," she said, "Moses' mother put Moses in the little ark and let him go among the crocodiles." Now that I didn't want to hear. Suddenly all the nice boys that Judy knew took on the shape of crocodiles! Then Margaret told me she would be like Miriam for me. She would stand watch on the riverbank in prayer. In essence, Margaret said to me, "Give me your child." And from that day to this she has carried my child to the upper room and prayed for her.

A few months after this incident, I received a package through the mail. It contained a little crocodile with its mouth tied up. "That's what prayer does," said the card!

Can you think of a mother in need, a father in trouble, a friend in dire distress with a child in a rehabilitation center? Why not contact them and say, "Give me your child." There are plenty of empty places on the riverbank today, waiting for watchers. A good thing to do is to pray about it. Ask the Lord which child is yours to pray for. Then make a commitment to that child. I sometimes ask for a photo to keep in my journal that reminds me to pray.

So Elijah learned to pray at Tishbe, to rest at Kerith, and to raise the dead at Zarephath! Now we can learn to pray such prayers — not prayers that will raise the physically dead but that will do something much more difficult. We can learn to pray effectively for the spiritually dead. It will take a lot of trust and the ability to believe when there is a dead child in your arms. But learn to climb those stairs to your upper room.

God gifts some of us to live in Zarephath. He trusts us with the privilege of praying "up close and personal". There is nothing that does you quite as much good as living in the heart of an unregenerate family and being trusted with the prayer work for them. These sorts of situations keep you on your knees. A woman said to me, "I have prayed less since I have had the privilege of living in a regenerate family than when I was home with my own beloved unbelievers." There's no way you can get lazy when you are living with the widow of Zarephath.

KEEPING UP THE PRAYERS

So what happened next? Once the boy was well, did the prayers stop? Not at all. I'm certain that they intensified. This was just the beginning of the battle. Remember, the devil had lost a soul.

After he'd raised the widow's son from the dead, Elijah remained in Zarephath for some time. The Bible says, "After a long time, in the third year, the word of the Lord came to Elijah" (1 Kings 18:1, NIV). The record doesn't state what Elijah did during that time, but if he followed the tradition of spiritual leaders before him, he used that three years to establish the victories he'd already won as well as plan for the battles ahead.

This too is part of prayer. When the Lord through Joshua encouraged the children of Israel to finish invading the land of Canaan, the Lord said to Joshua, "There are still very large areas of land to be taken over" (Josh. 13:1, NIV). He then gave instructions on how to finish the job. This was not to be at the expense of their past victories either. The land taken must be guarded, but the new land must be won. This has a parallel with the warfare we must engage in. In prayer we consolidate our gains while we plan future victories.

If we rest on our laurels, the devil will see his chance and try to undo our hard-won gains. How can we keep this from happening? We can work at the prayer of persistence. One way is to use a list. Get a book and take a page for each day. Write the name of each day at the top and then fill it in. You could pray for family on Monday, church concerns on Tuesday, widows of Zarephath on Wednesday, children among the crocodiles on Thursday, missions on Friday, and yourself on Saturday. Leave Sunday for anything the Lord brings to mind. This is just an idea to get you going. Don't let the list control you; you control the list.

The whole family can compile this sort of list over a mealtime. So as well as having a personal list, you can have a family list. Let the kids take part in making it and using it in their prayer. Children love to pray, especially for other children. We used a photo album at the table. We all threw pictures of our friends in there along with prayer — worthy items of interest such as a newspaper clipping about a lost child or trouble in the local schools. We didn't use the book every time we prayed, but we did use it consistently, and the children got used to it and looked forward to our family prayers.

When some of our grandchildren were in a stressful situation one time, I shared their problem with a friend at the other end of the country. She in turn shared it with her children. They took a photo of the kids I had sent and put it on the fridge. Each morning before they went to school they prayed for them together. There were four children in that family, as there were in ours, and one day one of their kids said, "Hey, Dad and Mom, why don't we each take on the kid who is nearest to our age?" And so they did, praying diligently until the trouble had passed. But the thing that delighted me most was that they so loved praying for our children that they didn't want to stop once the situation was better. So they continued. And what a blessing that has been, as the ground gained has been consolidated and we have developed a wonderful prayer connection with a great bunch of kids far away. Kids love to pray for kids, so involve them.

SPENDING TIME IN THE UPPER ROOM

The upper room in which Elijah brought the boy back to life has come to represent for me important principles of prayer. So let's talk about the upper room for a moment.

Prayer Involves Honesty

Our upper room is, first of all, a place to be honest. As we lay out that lifeless situation before God, we cry out to him. Elijah "cried out to the Lord" (1 Kings 17:20). A great, wrenching cry of grief and sorrow tore him apart. If we are going to pray effectively for the lost, for the spiritually dead, we need to ask a question: Do I care? I mean, really care?

When I first came to Christ, I cared. I really cared. I spent hours on my knees praying for my family. Great heart-wrenching sobs would tear me up as I realized how lost they were without Christ. But ask me now, forty years later, if I care as much, and I have to be honest and tell you, not always. But I also have to tell you that if I'm honest with God in the upper room and tell him how cold, how indifferent, how tired of praying I've become, he delights to ignite the fire again. But first I have to be honest.

Ask yourself, *What's the first thing I do in the upper room?* Can you hardly wait to climb the stairs to get there and go to work? Is your heart full and are your arms heavy with the weight of the one you are carrying? Do you cry out, or merely whimper? Whimpering will not do it!

I often think of a favorite hymn that was popular when I came to the Lord. One of the verses said:

> *Do you know that souls are dying, do you care?*
> *Children lost and voices crying, do you care?*
> *Can you say with God's dear Son, not my will but thine be*
> *   done,*
> *Does it matter, does it matter, do you care?*

So first be honest, and ask God for the great cry of Elijah to be born in your heart.

Prayer Involves Boldness

After you are honest, you can become bold. You can go beyond the barriers you have set up in the past. Elijah "stretched himself out over the child" (1 Kings 17:21). Stretch yourself. Ask for things you have never asked for before. Reach up, and work at pushing yourself to believe that anything is possible with God. So often our God is too small, our faith is too weak, our will is too faint, and our heart is too cold. We are timid in God's presence, and he would have us be bold. Someone once said, "Attempt great things for God, expect great things from God."

I was young in the faith, but bold. One day I got on my knees and said, "Lord, use me to reach the young kids roaming the streets." I was already teaching them by day, and I began to work with them by night. One evening we had a team of young people out on the streets contacting any kid who would listen to them.

I've already mentioned the huge dance hall where so many kids hung out. It was called the Floral Hall. There were literally hundreds of young people in there who needed Christ. I stood outside praying for the courage to go in. The courage never came, so I went in without it and found myself talking to the manager. Now came the bold part. I certainly didn't feel bold, and my inclination was to pray "get me out of here" prayers.

However at that very moment, I realized that the Lord was waiting for something bold. I thought about Peter walking on the water and how Jesus sounded really disappointed when Peter took his eyes off him and began sinking in his unbelief. I didn't want Jesus to be disappointed in me, so I tried to think of what would be the boldest course of action.

"Please, can I have your platform during the intermission?" I screamed above the din of the wild band. Secretly I was appalled. *What if he said yes?* He did! Then he asked, interested, "What do you want to do up there?" *It's all right being bold, Lord,* I complained, *but look where it's got me.*

Suddenly I knew what to do, and I knew what to say — I ended up talking to about one thousand kids for about ten minutes. I told them of a God who loved them, a Christ who died for them, and the way to have a friend who would never let them down. When it was over, my knees were shaking and I felt sick! Yet I had the strangest exhilaration inside. I'd walked on water, and I hadn't sunk! There is such a thing as holy boldness, and it comes when you exercise faith through prayer.

The great thing about the upper room is that it is portable. As I stood outside that dance hall, I was actually climbing the stairs to my own prayer room. Wherever you are, there is an upper room. If you will climb those stairs often, you will bring many an answered prayer to some grieving person.

Revealing to Others the One Who Answers Prayer

It was answered prayer that convinced the widow that the Lord truly spoke through Elijah. "Now I know for sure that you are a man of God," she said, "and that the Lord truly speaks through you" (1 Kings 17:24). I am not saying that we have to bring about a resurrection before people will believe, but I am saying that we can boldly ask for whatever it will take to convince people of the truth.

It took two things to win the widow. First, she needed to believe that Elijah was a man of God. His life had to speak before she would listen. Elijah's challenge was to live a consistently holy life. An elderly woman was asked whose preaching had converted her. "Nobody's preaching," she replied. "It was Aunt Mary's practicin'!" How many of us have been alerted to the gospel through the lifestyle of a friend or colleague?

When I was in college, I noticed a beautiful girl who seemed to excel at everything she did. She was our student-body president, and she possessed serenity that I envied. What was her secret? One day I was asked to take a note to her room. I knocked on the door but didn't wait for a reply. I rather rudely burst into her room. It was then I discovered her secret. She was on her knees with an open Bible on the bed in front of her. I was shocked. In this day and age, what did she think she was doing? To my surprise, she stayed there, smiled at me serenely, and asked me what she could do for me. I mumbled something and got myself out of there as quickly as I could. What could she do for me? She had already done it. She had shown me whose she was and whom she served. Later, if people asked me whose preaching had converted me, I would be able to say, "Nobody's preaching, it was Grace's practicin'." Elijah practiced his faith day after day, and the widow took note.

Second, the widow came to believe that the words Elijah spoke were God's words. She saw the power in them. As she took her boy out of Elijah's arms, she thought of all the prayers he had prayed for her child, asking his God to restore the boy's life and health. Well, here the boy was, alive and well. I'm sure that, even if the widow hadn't overheard Elijah's prayers in that room, once her son was restored she asked the prophet, "What did you say to bring this about?" If Elijah's prayers were so true, then all the other things he had been telling her must be true too.

As the widow began her walk of faith, I have no doubt there was a change of lifestyle and a practicing of faith in Jehovah. Among her new disciplines would probably be the establishing of her own upper room. She, like you and me thousands of years later, would establish a place, take the time, and make the effort to climb up to God and do the work of prayer. Who knows how many children of Baal will be in heaven because of her?

෴

A PRAYER FOR SICK CHILDREN

O God, you are the heavenly Parent,
the one who as a father watched your child
upon the cross and heard his cry for comfort.
You had the power to help and yet withheld your hand,
that we who watch the suffering may be the better.

Those of us who believe in you
know you as a suffering God,
and so we lean our heads upon your breast
and say that it helps to know — that you know.

O God, you are the Helper,
touched by the very feelings of our infirmities, you say.
Help us with the art of saying the right thing —
that those of us who do not naturally have a tongue of silver
may make rich those who know the poverty of ill health.

And you who are the one in heaven
who reveals the secrets of all mysteries,
roll the stone of ignorance aside.
Show the doctors secrets of the resurrection —
life from death!
Oh, lay down the giant of childhood sickness.

O God, you are the Healer,
promising bruised reeds that you shall not break
and smoking flax that you shall not quench.
We pray now for all persons in this case.
Touch them, Lord —
bring your healing hand low to their pain.
Do your work, show your heart,
hear us, help us, heal us.
Amen.

Discussion or Journal

1. Reread 1 Kings 17:17–24.
2. Do you think Elijah showed a lack of faith by asking God why?
3. What does the phrase "Give me your child" mean in your life today? Share an incident when people have prayed for your children or when you have prayed for theirs.
4. Read Ruth Bell Graham's poem on page 64. Take a moment to commit it to memory. It may help you in trouble. What does it mean to lay our questions at God's feet?
5. What did you learn about the upper room? Is it hard to be honest with God? Is it hard to be bold?
6. What do you do about wandering thoughts? Make a list of ten good ideas on how to deal with them.
7. Reread the verse about the widow's conversion (1 Kings 17:24). What impresses you about her statement to Elijah?

Time to Pray

1. Imagine yourself in Elijah's upper room. Pray some honest prayers.
2. Make a mental list of children in trouble. Pray for them.
3. Pray some really bold prayers.

4. Spend time asking God to help you care more about the lost.

To Do on Your Own
1. Read 1 Kings 18:16–40.
2. Think of a prayer God has answered. Don't stop praying about the situation. Continue to pray in order to keep the spiritual advantages you have won.

Notes and Ideas

CHAPTER FIVE

TAKING ON THE ENEMY

―――――――――― ❧ ――――――――――

AFTER A LONG TIME, IN THE THIRD YEAR IN FACT, IT WAS time for Elijah to leave Zeraphath. The Lord spoke to Elijah and said, "Go and present yourself to Ahab, and I will send rain on the land" (1 Kings 18:1, NIV). I can imagine that this was welcome news to Elijah, although the daily doings of the little family must have been a bit of security for him. Anyway, the Bible says simply, "So Elijah went to present himself to Ahab" (1 Kings 18:2, NIV). Just like that. What a lesson in obedience. After all, Ahab had been trying to find and kill Elijah for three years. But Elijah packed up his meager belongings and went. Maybe after being cared for by ravens and then a widow, he wasn't going to worry anymore about his safety.

God had the whole thing figured out. He knew that Ahab and his right-hand man, Obadiah, were out looking for water for their thirsty cattle. So he arranged for Elijah to be coming around the same bush as Obadiah. When Obadiah saw Elijah, he was amazed, "Is it really you, my lord Elijah?" he spluttered. "Yes," said Elijah. "Go tell your master, 'Elijah is here'" (1 Kings 18:7–8). After a bit of persuading, Obadiah complied.

Ahab's approach was aggressive: "Is that you, you troubler of Israel?" he said. "I have not made trouble for Israel," Elijah said. "But you and your father's family have" (1 Kings 18:17–18, NIV). Whereupon he told Ahab to go home and round up the prophets of Baal and all the people and bring them to Mount Carmel. I'm quite sure he didn't tell the king what he was going to do, but Ahab probably co-operated out of desperation for rain. So Ahab sent word throughout all Israel and assembled the prophets on Mount Carmel. The great contest was about to begin.

I can imagine that Elijah wondered how Ahab would approach his wife with the news that he had been told to bring all Israel to Mount Carmel. Perhaps he lied to her, or maybe she was out shopping when he arrived back home. Anyway, he dutifully rounded up the prophets of Baal and "sent word throughout all Israel" that they should make their way to meet Elijah (1 Kings 18:20, NIV).

THE APPEAL OF SITTING ON THE FENCE

Elijah knew he was living in a war zone. There was a fight between God and Satan, between good and evil, going on. Do we know that we are living in a war zone too? Someone hates us, and someone loves us. A higher power would call us to higher things, and a lower power would lead us to self-destruction. You and I, as surely as Elijah, are facing a very real enemy. Are we "prayed up" and ready for the battle? Elijah was well aware of the forces of evil behind the queen and her nefarious prophets, and he took them on in the name of the Lord. We in our generation must learn, also, to take on our battles in the name of the Lord.

Once the people arrived, Elijah didn't beat around the bush. He got right to the point. When we get a chance to get a hearing with neighbors or friends, at home or in the workplace, we need to take the opportunity as Elijah did. "How long will you waver between two opinions?" he asked the people. "If the Lord is God, follow him; but if Baal is God, follow him" (1 Kings 18:21, NIV). To us, reading this account and knowing the end, it seems like a simple choice.

But the people stayed silent, waiting and watching. They were sitting on the fence. When we are living in a war zone, we need to be aware that Satan is intent on keeping the fence occupied. He will do all he can to neutralize people's faith. To get people to waver, to sit on the fence in indecision, is to keep them out of the battle.

There are many reasons people sit on the fence today. Some stay there out of fear. Perhaps they are married to Jezebel! Ahab was certainly sitting on the fence, and we might assume that Jezebel was a big factor in keeping him there! Others stay silent because they are confused. Maybe they think it is arrogant to believe that there is only one true God and only one way to heaven. They think that other religions might have something to offer, or else there wouldn't be so many different religions out there. Sometimes people would rather think that there are many options to choose from.

Elijah knew he had to get Israel off the fence, so he proposed a very simple test. He presented them with this: Let's see which god answers prayer. Now this made good sense to the people. What sort of god was worth his salt if he couldn't answer prayer?

THE GREAT ATTRACTION OF ANSWERED PRAYER

I have traveled the world and found people on every continent who pray. It is a fact that there is a growing number of people who do not believe in any sort of god; this is an alarmingly large group. But still, the majority of people believe in something. They seem to know that Someone out there is bigger and more powerful than they are. It was a stroke of genius for Elijah to tap into such a common belief. Most people prayed, or at the very least they knew they should pray, and so they readily accepted a contest that would reveal the true answerer of prayer.

If you ever find yourself getting nowhere when you are witnessing to someone, try sharing some answers to prayer. People who pray want their prayers answered. Even people who are not in dire distress would like to find what seems to them the magic formula. Of course, we know that prayer is not a matter of getting God to do what we want him to do but rather one of God getting us to do what he wants us to do. But the topic of answered prayer can open up an opportunity to explain the gospel.

I was on a plane going to the East Coast. It was a long flight, and I was just settling down to read when the well-dressed man by my side said, "It's hot in here. I can't wait to get to my house on the beach." He then proceeded to tell me all about this house and that house of his, this boat and that boat, this vacation and that vacation. It was going to be a very long flight! Then it was as if the Lord nudged me and said, "Tell him about me." "He wouldn't be interested, Lord," I replied confidently. "Haven't you noticed, he's a self-made man who worships his creator!" "True," the Lord replied, "but how do you know he wouldn't worship me instead of himself if he ever got to hear the truth?"

Let me pause just long enough to point out that this inner conversation I was having with the Lord was prayer. I was having a dialog with the Almighty. This sort of praying is like a conversation in your mind. This is the sort of thing that must have been going on at Mount Carmel. As the situation unfolded, God had a "mind talk" with his servant Elijah, and his servant talked back to him in his thoughts. I love this sort of conversation with God. This kind of prayer can go on all day long.

The man on the plane talked happily about himself almost all the way to our destination. I listened as well as I could, figuring he would have to run out of words and give me a turn! At last he turned to me and said, "And what do you do?" I was delighted to tell him and in the course of my explanation managed to explain why I do what I do.

"Well," he responded, "some people need God, but my life is just fine as it is."

"Wouldn't you like it to be better?" I asked.

"Everyone would like it to be better," he concluded, "however good they have it."

"Then let me tell you how it could be better."

Talking very fast as we began to land, I recounted true stories of answered prayer. "Do you mind my asking you if you pray?" I ventured to inquire as we collected our things.

"Not very often," he admitted.

"Life will be better even than it is when you do."

"I wouldn't know where to start."

"Start at the beginning," I suggested.

As we walked down to the baggage claim area, I told him where the beginning was. He would need to examine the Christian's claims about Jesus, stop wavering between two opinions, and make a decision one way or another. In essence, I told him, "If the Lord be God, then serve him, but if Baal (or the mighty dollar), then serve him." He left then. But I pray on for him whenever the Lord brings him to mind. I pray that one day he will pray a prayer of faith and, finding that prayer works, give his life to the Lord. Yes, people really do believe that any gods worth their salt will be able to answer their people's prayers. And when people see prayers answered, they are often willing to cast their vote for the God who did the answering.

THE BUILDING OF ALTARS

Elijah turned his attention to the prophets of Baal. He told them to go ahead and build an altar. He would do the same. Then they would take a sacrifice and offer it to their respective gods. The god who answered by sending fire down to burn up the sacrifice would be declared the winner. Remember that the people had been told that Baal, not Jehovah, was the source of the spring and autumn rains. Surely their god would send the storm and the lightning to honor the prayers of his people? So the prophets set to work.

After the altars had been built, the prophets of Baal made their sacrifice and began prophesying and working themselves into a frenzy, cutting themselves with knives as was their habit. Then they prayed to their god. "They called on the name of Baal all morning, shouting, 'O Baal, answer us.'" I think that the next words are some of the saddest in the Bible: "But there was no reply of any kind" (1 Kings 18:26).

Elijah told the people of Israel to come closer, so they could see what he was doing. They watched as he took twelve stones, one for each of the tribes of Israel, and restored the altar of the Lord. (Apparently Jezebel had been on a rampage, destroying the altars of the Lord throughout the land.) What Elijah was doing was very important. The people knew that those altars represented Israel's relationship with Jehovah, a relationship that had been violated over and over again. In fact, the people's relationship with their Maker was in ruins too. Elijah's actions were not lost on them. They knew he was inviting them to repair their own altar. In other words, it was "sorry" time, time to repent and turn back to God.

What a picture! Do you and I need to spend time repairing the altar of the Lord? Is your relationship with God in ruins? Did you violate your covenant with God and have you been living with the results? Maybe you made a promise to love and serve the Lord years ago, yet you haven't darkened the door of a church for years. Perhaps it's time to roll up your sleeves and start to collect those stones that represent your broken relationship with God. In the next chapter, we will explore this matter of repairing the altar in more detail.

THE CONFIDENCE OF KNOWING THE ONE TRUE GOD

I have been in many countries and watched people pray. And there have been incantations, a lot of hocus-pocus, and genuine though misplaced faith in gods of wood and stone. But it isn't the amount of faith you have that makes the difference. It's the object of your faith that matters.

Stuart and I live in a country area on a small fishing lake. It's weedy and reedy and is pretty shallow. In the winter it freezes over. It is called Henrietta Lake after a young girl who put all her faith in very thin ice and drowned by faith. If she had only put a tiny bit of faith in very thick ice she would have been saved by faith. It's not the amount of faith you have but the object of it that makes the difference. My heart goes out to people all over the world who are drowning by faith in false gods, all the more because I know where they could get their help if they only knew the Lord.

Elijah, facing off with the prophets of Baal, egged them on. He began taunting them. "'You'll have to shout louder,' he scoffed, 'for surely he is a god! Perhaps he is deep in thought, or he is relieving himself. Or maybe he is away on a trip, or he is asleep and needs to be wakened!'" (1 Kings 18:27).

You can imagine how this incensed the prophets of Baal. "So they shouted louder, and following their normal custom, they cut themselves with knives and swords until the blood gushed out. They raved all afternoon until the time of the evening sacrifice, but still there was no reply, no voice, no answer" (vv. 28–29).

When we are taking on the enemy, the first thing we have to do, after repairing our own relationship with the

Lord, is affirm our belief in the one true God. Speaking through the prophet Isaiah, the Lord says loudly and clearly, "I alone am God. There is no other God; there never has been and never will be. I am the Lord, and there is no other Savior." Then the Lord says, "You are witnesses that I am the only God.... From eternity to eternity I am God" (Isa. 43:10–13).

This was where Elijah started, and this is where we must start. As Elijah built his altar and made the sacrifice, he prayed aloud. This is what he prayed: "O Lord,... prove today that you are God in Israel and that I am your servant." And then again, "O Lord, answer me! Answer me so these people will know that you, O Lord, are God and that you have brought them back to yourself" (1 Kings 18:36–37).

The prayer that affirms that God is God in heaven above and on earth below is a prayer that God affirms. And when we pray that prayer for others, trusting God to convince those we pray for of his sovereignty, we can know that he will let the fire fall on our altar and the sacrifice we have prepared. Somehow, some way, he will answer that prayer. So when we are taking on the enemy, we must loudly declare that there is but one God and that he is the only Savior.

Then we need to stand up to the servants of the enemy. Elijah taunted them. He had no sympathy for the men who were decimating Israel's culture and faith. He boldly confronted them and challenged them to a contest. He knew he was on safe ground, because what he knew of the truth he knew to be the truth, and what he knew of the power of God he knew to be superior to all the power of the enemy.

I'm sure that Elijah was well aware of Satan's existence and that his cohorts could do much magic. But only God can do a miracle. And there was one thing that the prophets of Baal could certainly not do and that was answer their own prayers. No matter how much hocus-pocus they used, Satan could not answer prayer; only God could do that. So these things gave Elijah boldness to confront error in the name of the Lord. Knowing you are right gives you holy boldness. We are not half right but all right when it comes to the Word of God. It is not arrogant to believe the truth; it is rather arrogant not to believe it.

The thing that gave me holy boldness in our youth mission days was the belief that we were right and that our young opponents were wrong or perhaps just ignorant of the truth. It was such faith in the Word of the Lord that drove Elijah to take on the prophets of Baal single-handedly.

THE ASSURANCE OF KNOWING GOD'S WORD AND WILL
Elijah readied himself for the prayer of faith that would bring the fire to consume the sacrifice. He knew he was praying in response to what God had revealed. If we are going to see the fire fall, we must be intellectually convinced of the revealed will of God through his Word. We cannot arbitrarily decide to take some parts as truth and ignore others.

In his business days, my husband lived in a YMCA in Manchester, England. He got to know a young student there who had great difficulty believing the miracles of the Bible. He was not a believer, and Stuart began meeting with him to talk about the Bible and about faith. In the end, Stuart handed the young man a Bible and said, "Here you are, John. Here's a Bible and a pair of scissors — go and cut out all the bits you can't believe."

"Oh," John replied, "I couldn't cut the Bible."

"You've been cutting it to bits with your tongue," Stuart replied, "so what's the difference?"

John went away, and a few days later, he returned with a small portion of the Bible Stuart had given him. "Now let me tell you what you have in your hand," said my husband. "You have a God that John can understand. What sort of a God is that?" John eventually came to faith in the God of the Bible, a God who was supernatural and who was bigger than he. There is no way we will see the Lord in action if we have a skeptical view of the Scriptures. Belief and power go together.

THE PREREQUISITES TO POWER

F. B. Meyer, a devotional writer, said, "There is nothing the church needs more today than spiritual power, and there is nothing we can have so easily if only we are prepared to pay the price." So there are requirements of us if we wish to see God's power demonstrated in our prayers.

We can use Elijah's situation on Mount Carmel to explore the requirements for powerful prayers. We see that Elijah first prepared the altar. Then he made his sacrifice. Then he trusted God. I'm giving names to these three actions: repentance, surrender, and faith.

The first requirement is that we repair our altar. This is so important that I have spent all of chapter 6 discussing the different stones in our altars that might need to be repaired and put back in place. And in chapter 7, we will look more closely at surrender and faith. For now, however, let's be certain we understand repentance.

THE ESSENCE OF REPENTANCE

When I was a new believer, the girl who led me to Christ told me to "keep short accounts with God". What she meant by that was that I should not let things pile up but try to repent as I went through the day.

"A glance heavenward will do it, Jill," she advised. "Just say, 'Oops, Father, there I go again! I'm truly sorry.' This way you keep the slate clean and don't pile up a huge heap of rubbish by the end of the day." Even after forty years of following Christ, I still need to say oops throughout the day — and at the end of it as well.

All those years ago, my spiritual advisor told me that at night I should "kneel down and, starting at the beginning of the day, go over all you did and all you said, piece by piece, saying sorry as you go along". This may sound elementary, but I still use that little exercise, and it works well. This way you really keep short accounts with God. Repentance is simply this: agreeing with God about all the things you've done that you shouldn't have done and all the things you haven't done that you should have done, and asking him to forgive you.

Some people might say, "I thought my sins were dealt with when I prayed the sinner's prayer." In a sense that is true. If you have asked Christ to come into your life, all your sin — past, present, and future — has been forgiven.

Think of Jesus' parable of the Prodigal Son. Here was a boy who rebelled, left home, and went wild. After he had ruined his life, he "finally came to his senses" and repented (Luke 15:17). He went home, admitted his sin, and cast himself on his father's mercy.

This is a picture we can all relate to. We need to take that long walk home every day of our lives! Remember that God's blood runs in our veins. Blood being thicker than water, and especially divine blood, we must not hesitate to say to our Father, anytime of the day or night, "Father, I have sinned against both heaven and you, and I am no longer worthy of being called your son" (Luke 15:18–19).

I'm sure this experience made the son sensitive to sin in his life thereafter. I can see him keeping short accounts with his father after this experience, can't you? Perhaps we need to look into our own lives and ask ourselves a question: Do I keep short accounts with God? If we don't make this a habit, we will find God distancing himself from us.

Something that will help us to understand how important it is to be forgiven on an ongoing basis, is to reflect on the enormous cost to Christ to forgive all our sins in the first place. Has the enormity of our sin ever sunk in? Have we been forgiven much? Jesus said of the sinful woman in Luke 7:47, "Therefore, I tell you, her many sins have been forgiven — for she loved much. But he who has been forgiven little loves little" (NIV). Maybe we don't see our sins as so very bad.

Sometimes those who have been brought up in Christian homes and have led somewhat sheltered lives find repentance difficult. They can't think of things to be really sorry about. They haven't been allowed to rebel. They haven't gotten drunk or taken drugs. They don't swear or curse, and they are respectful to their families. So what do they have to be sorry about?

We have too little concept of what the "big sins" really are. God hates pride, for example. He despises selfishness. He especially rebukes spiritual smugness, or counting ourselves superior to others. He has forbidden us to covet anything. Coveting means saying, "I want what she's got." We are to be content with the things God has given us, so it is a sin to be full of discontent. When we begin to figure out what sin really is — a coming short of the perfection that God requires — then repentance makes sense to everybody, even those of us who have lived seemingly "good" lives.

Repairing the altar of the Lord represents repairing our covenant relationship with God, and that is accomplished by practicing an attitude of "sorry", on a moment-by-moment basis. Elijah prayed about sins of commission and sins of omission, and we need to do that too. The children of Israel had deliberately broken down the altars of the Lord, and they had intentionally disobeyed many of his command-ments. But they had also omitted loving the Lord their God with all their heart, soul, mind, and strength. They had most certainly failed to love their neighbors as themselves. (See

Luke 10:27, where Jesus summed up what God had asked of people.)

To love as God loves is the first commandment. If I love as God loves, then I am primarily concerned for the well-being of others, irrespective of the cost to myself. Think about it. If we only pray about ourselves, and seldom put others' prayer needs first, we sin!

Samuel said this very thing to the rebellious children of Israel: "As for me, I will certainly not sin against the Lord by ending my prayers for you" (1 Sam. 12:23). As we kneel at God's feet at the end of the day, we can ask him to show us our sins of commission and sins of omission. When he brings them to our minds, we can start by calling things by their real names. Just as it is a good exercise to praise God by counting our blessings one by one, so it is a helpful exercise to name our sins one by one. Be specific. Spell it out. And God will hear your confession and cleanse you from all sin.

Sin bars the door to the fullness of the Holy Spirit. Open your heart and let him expose anything that may be there that prevents him from working in your life. Write down all the instances you can remember, when you have received favors from God, for which you have never exercised gratitude. How many cases can you remember? The numerous mercies you have received with a half thankful heart. Go to your knees and confess them one by one to God, and ask for forgiveness (*Charles Finney on Spiritual Power*, Lance Wubbels, ed.).

I remember seeing my lack of prayer for others as something so much worse than mere neglect. Yet if I believe the best thing I can do for others is to pray for them, then I can admit that a lack of prayer is a sin of omission. I came to realize this when my husband was at the other end of the world. Out of sight, out of mind, they say. But it has never been like that for us. One habit we both established early in our married life was that of continual prayer for each other. Once reunited, we would share times we felt constrained to pray, only to find that at that particular moment things had not been going well or a specific need had arisen that required special grace or patience. Both of us testified to a strengthening here or a solution there that often amazed us.

Some friends, who are missionaries, sent me a poem written by a friend. The friend was a Bible translator who worked in a faraway place. He was married, and their work necessitated lengthy separations from each other. A verse of Scripture that seemed particularly appropriate was Genesis 31:49: "May the Lord keep watch between you and me when we are away from each other" (NIV). This led to a poem:

Helping together,
Helping together so far apart! Long distances dividing.
And loving words pass not our hearts between,
Nor know we each the many things betiding,
Nor on each other comforted may lean.
But we may pray with strong and holy pleading,
And live so that our pleadings must prevail:
And He who knoweth well what each is needing,
Can guide us what to ask, to help avail.
And at the end, when safely home in glory,
When prayers and needs have changed for wonders new,
How sweet, how blest, if we may read the story,
Of how each helped to pray each other through!

J. Danson Smith

It's a new discipline to think of omitting to do something as a sin. But in the words of the Anglican confession, "We have left undone those things which we ought to have done; and we have done those things which we ought not to have done; and there is no health in us. But thou, O Lord, have mercy upon us, miserable offenders. Spare thou those, O God, who confess their faults." If I am ungrateful, I need to repair my altar. If I neglect to pray at all or neglect to pray for someone I love that I have promised to pray for, I need to ask God's forgiveness.

All sin cuts us off from God's fullness, power, and love. But "because of the Lord's great love we are not consumed, for his compassions never fail. They are new every morning; great is your faithfulness" (Lam. 3:22–23, NIV). As we get up early in the morning, we can know we face a new day with the slate wiped clean. We can face a new day in a new way because we have been busy repairing our altar, using our little trowel of prayer, before we ever put our head on the pillow at night. Through prayer, the power of repentance operates deep down inside, renewing the frayed edges of our souls.

What do you know about this aspect of the devotional life? Do you, with the little boy who struggled with this say, "I find 'sorry' hard!" Don't be discouraged. "Sorry", is hard for all of us. Our unsorry hearts have to be taught by the Holy Spirit how to be sorry. But he is more than willing to be our teacher. After all, this is one of his most necessary works in our lives.

If we are to take on the enemy of our souls, namely, the devil, we can be assured that the one word he hates to hear us utter is *sorry*. He will work against us constantly, trying to distract us from the work of repentance. He will suggest all sorts of reasons God is unreasonable to expect that little word to come out of our mouths — and our deceitful hearts will want to believe him. But God will pay attention to a truly contrite heart. He is close to those who are humble in spirit, and he hears and answers the truly sorry ones.

Does the pattern of our prayers reflect adequate repentance? Elijah was well aware he was in an unseen battle with an enemy far too strong for him. But he used the weapons of warfare supplied by the Spirit and fought on.

❧

A Prayer for God to Move Us into Action

Lord, where can we go but to you? We have no one in heaven beside you and no one on earth with your grand ability to touch our spirits, lift our mood, bless our kids, stick us back together again when we fall apart, or sew a torn relationship into place.

We wonder what you see in this wild world of ours that we cannot.
A crowd of cowards?
A sea of sin?
A morass of people picking and clawing at each other?
Hurt husbands or rejected wives who find it difficult to look their neighbors in the face?

Or do you perhaps see those of us who are celebrating —
the "I have need of nothing" individuals, the "keep your religion, I have mine" group? The cynic or the scoffer, or even little children capable of huge injustice on their own sweet level?

See, Lord, we are all here together
in this your hurting world.
Have mercy on us all.

Nudge us into your will and away from our wants. Reduce us to size. Show us your mighty arm! Carry our sin away and move us into action that we may make a bold stand, a walking statement that will tell this needy world — that Jesus is our public choice!

We pray this, dear Lord:
that Calvary may be worthwhile.
Amen.

Discussion or Journal

1. Why do you think people waver between two opinions? Why can't we allow them to do this?
2. Do we stay silent when we get an opportunity to challenge people who are sitting on the fence? Why?
3. What have been some definite answers to your prayers? Have you ever shared these with anyone, and did this give you a further opportunity to share your faith?
4. What did the twelve stones of the altar represent? What was symbolic about Elijah's repairing it?
5. What does it mean for us to repair the altar of the Lord?
6. Where do we find holy boldness? Give examples from your own experience.
7. What does it mean to keep short accounts with God?
8. What are sins of commission and sins of omission? Discuss sins of omission. Write a "sorry" prayer for a sin of omission.

Time to Pray

1. Get alone and beginning with the start of the day, go over it piece by piece. As you go along this review, tell God you're sorry for the sins that come to mind. Thank God for hearing your confession and forgiving you.

2. Read Luke 15:18–20. Use the son's words to his father to express your feelings. Then read the father's words to his son and claim them for yourself.

3. Make a list of your sins of omission today. Confess them.

To Do on Your Own

Read Daniel 9. Work through it, making a list of the things you, too, should repent of. Pray for your people, using Daniel's words. Pray for yourself.

Notes and Ideas

CHAPTER SIX

PUTTING THINGS IN PLACE

———⟨⟩———

THE PICTURE OF REBUILDING THE ALTAR OF THE LORD is a helpful one. As we build our lives, as God would have us build them, we will find our prayers getting to be more and more effective. There are two lines in J. Danson Smith's poem on page 90 that merit another look:

> *But we pray with strong and holy pleading,*
> *And live so that our pleadings must prevail.*

As we live "so that our pleadings must prevail", we will find that our prayers work. This is not to say that we have to be perfect. But we need to be working at becoming perfectly obedient to the ongoing work of the Holy Spirit in our lives.

When you think of Elijah, you think of a holy man. He was a man certainly flawed, yet he was determined to let God deal with the flaws in his life on an ongoing basis. Those who deliberately refuse to allow the Lord to deal with their flaws will find their prayer lives flawed as well. So how do we do this? How do we recognize that the altar needs repairing? How do we pick up the stones of the altar and put them back in place? Why don't we rebuild the altar together?

When I was thinking of the ways I could illustrate this point, I drew myself an altar on a piece of paper and filled in the stones.

I tried to think of elements of my relationship with God that needed to be in place so that my prayers would not be hindered. That I might live "so that my pleadings must prevail". My altar will not be your altar, and your altar will not be my altar. Some elements will be the same for all of us, but since we are very different people, some stones are bound to be different. Let's examine some of the elements we all share.

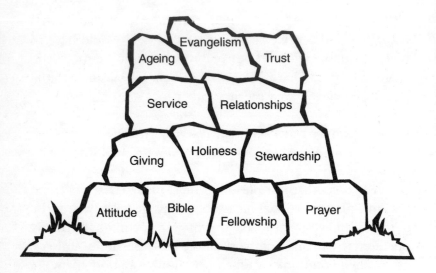

ATTITUDE

Let's begin with attitude. Attitude makes a big difference. It can mean the difference between growth and stagnation in the Christian life. You can do anything with a child who has a good attitude. I remember my mother asking me to come and help her in the kitchen. I was thirteen at the time, and my attitude stank. After hearing a second demand from the vicinity of the kitchen, I reluctantly heaved myself up off the couch and arrived by my mother's side like a small tornado. She took one look at my face and said, "Off you go. I'd rather do without your help than have a face like that helping me." Maybe God feels the same way when he sees our attitude showing! Some of us live our Christian lives like sulky thirteen-year-olds. We have a face like thunder and an attitude to match.

Elijah never gives me the impression of being a reluctant servant of the Lord. Rather, I see him with a passion to please, a heart for the lost, and a "gratitude attitude". As I repair the altar of the Lord and put the stones back in place, I must first attend to my attitude. Attitude is a question of choice.

Visiting a youth center one day, I was talking to the leader in his office. Suddenly the door opened, and a woman appeared wielding a broom. She furiously began sweeping out the office as if she had a personal vendetta against dust and dirt! We hastily moved out of her way, and she whisked out of the place in a minute. Later on I came across her attacking another area of the house in like manner, and I smiled and greeted her. "What a wonderful job you are doing," I commented. There was a flashing glance in my direction, and then the woman resumed her furious sweeping. As I passed by, I heard her mutter, "I try to do my work to the glory of God!"

This woman was obviously an unhappy servant of the Lord. But I couldn't help thinking of the many times the Lord greeted me at my work only to receive such a surly response. It is all too common to furiously "do our work to the glory of God" with a surly soul. God can do without that. Attitude is sweetened in the prayer room. He who said, "The Son of man came not to be served but to serve" wants to develop a servant spirit in our hearts (Matt. 20:28, RSV).

The Bible

Then there is the Bible stone. Maturity in the way we understand and apply God's Word is a worthy goal for every Christian. And such growth will undoubtedly affect a person's prayer life. We have already said that the Bible calls us to pray according to the will of God as revealed in the Word of God. It makes sense that the better we know the Bible, the better we'll know how to pray.

Try to find a system for reading the Bible. Once you have that in place, think as you read. Be on the lookout for the will of God in the text. Notice the commands in Scripture. Commands are usually things that God wants you to do. He wants you to do his will, and finding a command means that you have found something that is God's will. The Bible will instruct you in all dimensions of living effectively for God and his kingdom. As you become familiar with how God thinks and wants things done, you will find yourself deciding to follow the instructions of the Lord.

Some people find it helpful to read Scripture first and then pray through it. For example, you could read Psalm 23. Then you could take each verse and pray the ideas in it for someone. For example, "The Lord is my shepherd" (Ps. 23:1) may lead you to pray that he might be the shepherd to your friends and loved ones too.

The Bible also gives us the ingredients of effective prayer. How stupid it would be if I were baking a cake and I didn't bother with the instructions on the package! Just imagine what the cake would taste like if I presumed to throw in all my own ideas instead of following the directions on the label. Reading the Bible teaches me about the necessary ingredients of the Christian life, including how to pray prayers that work. Maturity in the Word is a choice in the same way that my attitude is a choice.

FELLOWSHIP

Fellowship is another essential ingredient of my life in Christ. I cannot fight the battle alone, nor am I meant to. The Lord does not appreciate pride in the person who thinks she can do this alone. We may have to do some of it alone, but it is God's good intention to pair us up with heart partners in the larger scheme of things. The disciples went out two by two for good reason, and we weak human beings need each other as well.

Personal friendships are one thing, but corporate friendship is another. The church is God's idea, not ours. When a church is functioning properly, people blossom and flourish like leaves on a tree. As I avail myself of the opportunities of life and service offered through my local church, things get put into place in my life.

But what if the church is not functioning properly? Many people are disillusioned with the church. Perhaps you are one of those people. Join a church anyway. Try to make sure a particular church body believes the Bible and teaches it. Ask for a statement of faith, and see if it rings true. Pray about it. Ask if the church is evangelical. Because every church is made up of imperfect people, every church is lacking in some way. But we need to get in there and get doing and try to contribute. Join a Bible study in the church's fellowship. Small groups are great for asking questions and finding answers. They're also good for developing friendships, and everyone needs Christian friends. God wants you in a fellowship of believers for your own good as well as theirs. You need each other. And it is in the church that you can begin to learn to participate in corporate prayer.

PRAYER

At first it may be difficult to pray aloud in front of people. Most people find it hard. There might be an "expert" in your prayer group who intimidates you. Don't let anyone rob you of the joy of talking with the Father along with your friends. Here are some basic rules that may help:

- Keep your words few and to the point.
- Remember that you are talking to God, not to the group.
- Speak naturally and simply, trying not to use King James English.
- Don't analyze your prayer when you are finished.

Another thing that may help you become more comfortable with praying out loud in a group is to practice in private. Practice praying on your own, alone in your room. It may seem strange at first, but it will really help you pray out loud with others.

Another reason it is good to join a church and a prayer group is that both will provide opportunities for you to serve God and others. God has gifted every Christian with gifts of service for the common good, and the church should help you discover your (and others') gifts, pray about them together, and put them to work. As you work corporately to serve the Lord in the church and outside its walls, your prayer life will develop. You will want to pray about the various activities you are engaged in and the ministries of the fellowship you belong to. The Bible says that we should not forsake the assembling of ourselves together (Heb. 10:25). Perhaps we should repair our altar at this point and take some determined steps to join a fellowship of Jesus' followers.

The personal devotional life is what the body of this book is all about, so I won't address this element here but will move on to the next tier of stones.

STEWARDSHIP

Stewardship spans two of the next elements of my life in Christ: Hilarity in giving and frugality in spending. Now these two things are all too often in sad need of repair in my life. Yet they constitute a very important part of my relationship with the Lord. Money — too much or too little — can so distract me from the business of serving the Lord that my prayers diminish in power in no time flat!

Having been brought up in affluence, I never really learned the true value of money as a girl. Then I married a bank inspector! Shortly after we were married, Stuart asked me to keep books. At first I thought he meant start a library! Then it dawned on me that he meant for me to write down everything I spent in columns and add it all up at the end of the week. This took a considerable toll on our relationship, as I could never get it right. At the bottom of the column where, apparently, other people wrote, "Balance", I wrote, "Left to Spend"! Exasperated, my usually patient husband would ask, "All right then, where is it?" To which I would reply, "I've spent it!"

God says that he "loves a cheerful giver" (2 Cor. 9:7, NIV). I need — now, as I did back then — to stop being an indulgent spender and become a generous giver instead. And I need to become responsible with the resources God provides.

Do I freely and gladly open my home to those in need? Do I lend my car to a man out of work, choosing to take public transportation instead? Do I give all year round or just when my emotions are heightened or when I'm asked to through an appeal letter or TV campaign? Do I raise my missions giving year by year, believing that God is no man's debtor? Am I miserly or generous with my time? Do I buy a camp holiday for a child who couldn't afford to go otherwise, or do I just look after my own? These are the questions God's Holy Spirit asks me all the time.

Putting the stones of our altar in place may mean addressing such "unreligious" matters as money. But only as we spend valuable time working on what needs attention — whether it is secular or spiritual — will we grow in grace and usefulness. All these things constitute a holy life. A holy life is not to be confused with a "holier than thou" life. A holy life is a life that pleases God. It is a life of humble, quick obedience and generous, glad service.

SERVICE

The stones on the next tier are of particular importance to me. The first has to do with my service gift. My service gift happens to be the gift of words. Putting things in place in order to live a more productive life for God includes examining how he has gifted me. God gifts the people of God with gifts of service. He intends that we discover what these gifts are, and he intends that we use them. As I practice my God-given skills for the good of the church and the world, I find my prayer life taking wings.

Not long after becoming a Christian, I discovered that my words mattered. People were listening to them. I had a general gift of words before my conversion, but after my conversion, my words seemed to be invested with a dynamism I had never known before. I was discovering my service gift. It was as if my words had wings! As I worshiped God in my personal devotional life, I noticed a direct correlation between my times of personal worship and the effectiveness of my words in the world in which I lived. One of the most significant poems I have written has to do with this very thing.

Give my words wings, Lord.
May they alight gently on the branches of men's minds
bending them to the winds of your will.

May they fly high enough to touch the lofty,
low enough to breathe the breath
of sweet encouragement upon the downcast soul.

Give my words wings, Lord.
May they fly swift and far,
winning the race with the words of the worldly wise
to the hearts of men.

Give my words wings, Lord.
See them now nesting
down at thy feet,
silenced into ecstasy,
home at last.

I discovered that if my words had not worshiped, they would never "win the race with the words of the worldly wise to the hearts of men". If I could learn to speak more to God about people than to people about God, the Lord would wing my words to many a heart. The more we exercise our spiritual gifts, the more we need to pray about them. Whatever our gifts are, prayer is a vital component of our service through those gifts.

When I think of my service gift and how often so little prayer goes into it, I am ashamed. It is just too easy to stand up and speak with a perfunctory nod in the direction of the Almighty. And the more you speak, the less you get on your knees about it. We may pay lip service to our relying on the Lord, but in fact we have moved away from dependence because we have acquired a little bit of expertise. If we do not function from helplessness and dependence on God, so much of our endeavor may be mere human effort rather than the dynamic work of the Holy Spirit.

There is a balance, of course. There was a time in my

life when I took pride in being almost incoherent with anxiety when I spoke. This, I felt, showed my dependence on God. However, my patient husband pointed out that I was almost impossible to listen to when I was in such a state. There needed to be a healthy dependence that mixed the awareness of my need for God's enabling with the confidence that he would indeed enable! That helped. I prayed about it and have been working on it ever since. Pray about your gifting all the time, so that you can keep things as they should be.

RELATIONSHIPS

I need to keep my relationships in good order. If my fellowship is broken with family or friends, or if I am out of sorts with my husband or have had words with my children, I need to speak to God about that as soon as possible. In fact, I have learned to almost have a three-way conversation going when things get heated. There will be no fire on my altar while things are out of sorts with my loved ones. "There I go again, Lord," I say as I lose my temper or am curt or impatient. "Please forgive me and help me to repair the damage," I pray — and am instantly heard.

There have been a few times I have called someone from the airport before boarding a flight to say, "Sorry, I didn't mean what I said; forgive me." My meetings go a whole lot better at the end of that plane trip. Caring for my relationships with my family and friends in all these ways helps to keep the channel open to God so that my prayers work.

TRUST

Then there is the matter of trust. The Lord delights in our confidence in him. He wants us to pray prayers that show him we believe he is a rewarder of those who seek him.

Little faith produces little result. I don't know about you, but I find it hard to trust. But I do know that, as a parent, I delight in my children coming boldly to me and confidently asking me for things, even if for good reason I need to refuse them. I love Elijah's boldness. "O Lord, answer me! Answer me," he cries (1 Kings 18:37), and God sends down fire from heaven.

AGING

Then there is the "aging" stone. This is a stone that often tumbles down the hillside and has to be put back firmly in place before my prayer life returns to normal. It is not a stone that only elderly people struggle with, either. You can get just as upset about your thirtieth birthday as about your eightieth! Sometimes I mourn the fact that, at my age, I will never translate the Bible into a foreign language so that some unreached people group can read the Word of God in their own heart language. I will never have the opportunity to go to Bible school now, either. There is not enough time left to me.

When I mourn these moments out loud, my husband usually says something like, "Jill, do you believe you were born at the right time?"

"Yes," I answer.

"Do you believe you are growing at the right speed?"

"Yes."

"Then," Stuart says cheerfully, "you'll be dead on time!" This relentless logic doesn't always work! But he is right. God's clocks keep perfect time, and when I trust him with my days and hours and know that, in fact, he has numbered my days, I can resume the work I've been given — and watch the fire fall. I heard retold a little story from the writer James Michener on this point.

When Michener was five, a farmer living at the end of

the lane hammered eight nails into the trunk of an aging, unproductive apple tree. That autumn a miracle happened. The tired old tree produced a bumper crop of juicy red apples. When James asked how this had happened, the farmer replied that hammering the rusty nails gave the tree a shock to remind it that its job was to produce apples.

In the 1980s, when Michener was nearly eighty, he had some nails hammered into his "trunk": heart surgery, vertigo, and a new left hip. And, like a sensible tree, he resolved to resume bearing fruit.

I may be slowed down by the aging process, but like "a sensible tree", I need to keep bearing fruit, no matter what particular nails have been hammered into my trunk. I am indeed just the right age in God's economy, and I can trust the Lord for everything. My job is to be righteous whatever my age, while God's job is to fill my life with his life and fruitfulness. Psalm 92:12–15, NIV says:

> The righteous will flourish like a palm tree, they will grow like a cedar of Lebanon; planted in the house of the Lord, they will flourish in the courts of our God. They will still bear fruit in old age, they will stay fresh and green, proclaiming, "The Lord is upright; he is my Rock, and there is no wickedness in him."

EVANGELISM

One last element of my life in Christ is evangelism. This is a stone that all too often requires attention. I could spend the remaining days of my life among Christians. It takes a huge effort on my part to make friends with unbelievers with a view to leading them to Christ. But to concentrate all of my energies toward nurturing believers removes me from a vital part of spiritual life. It also takes me off the cutting edge of prayer.

There is nothing quite like praying for people to come to Christ. And praying for our relatives and friends can lead us into an intensity that is not experienced in other forms of prayer. If we believe what we believe — that there is a heaven but also a hell and that good as well as bad people go there — we will pray. If we recognize the awful reality of lostness and what it means to be "without God, without Christ, and without hope", we will long to be on our faces before God about the matter.

When I first came to Christ, I couldn't stand the thought that those I loved were lost. While at college, I was always anxious to get alone and talk to the Lord about it. The lost condition of these loved ones was my waking thought. It occupied my mind throughout the day and worried me at night. I didn't have to discipline myself to have my "quiet time"; I carried those concerns with me all the time. For this reason I was into evangelism. The knowledge of people's spiritual danger drove me to my knees and kept me there.

But that concern also took up most of my spare time. How could I not have my friends' well-being uppermost in my thoughts, prayers, and actions? My recreational time became an opportunity for friendships to develop that could lead to conversations about the Lord I loved. Each course I took had the wonderful potential for interaction at a class level to state the principles I was now trying to live by.

One day my drama teacher handed out a new play to read. A quick glance told me it was a Greek tragedy. Parts were assigned, and I was asked to read the lead. It was a sad piece of literature, with little to commend it. However, it gave me a great chance to point out the hopelessness it engendered, and it enabled me to contrast the play's hopelessness with the hope of the Christian. This brought forth an outcry from my skeptical friends, and the whole of our class time was taken up with a debate on Christianity versus other faiths. Not knowing enough, I suspect I didn't fare too well on God's behalf, but the talk continued after the class, and at least one of those girls took time to consider the claims of Christ.

The next few days found me thinking and praying for that girl day and night. I shared the situation with some of my Christian friends, and we pledged to get up every morning to pray for her until she came to faith. It didn't take long, and soon she joined us in our early morning vigil to pray for friends of hers she was trying to bring to the Lord. That term saw dozens of girls in the college make professions of faith, as one by one they were prayed for, came to the Lord, and then joined the growing number of pray-ers on their knees in the prayer room. Nobody had to twist our arms to pray. Prayer was a perfectly natural outcome of a driving necessity to see our friends saved. Like Elijah, we could not stand to see people wavering between two opinions. Especially when we knew that to sit on a fence of indecision could mean spiritual disaster.

Motivation in our prayer life is a problem for many of us. For me, there is absolutely no problem when I allow the Lord to show me the realities of the truth about lostness. When prayer becomes hard for me, I look at that stone of evangelism and ask Jesus if I need to do a little (or a lot) of repair work.

So we must attend to our altars! Repentance means that we take our little trowel and get to work wherever "Jezebel" has wreaked havoc with our pile of stones. Morning, noon, and night our petitions must go up to God. Like the publican in Jesus' parable, we should continually be found beating our breasts and crying, "God, be merciful to me a sinner!" (Luke 18:13, NKJV). When Elijah symbolically repaired the altar of the Lord, he gave us an example we can — and should — follow. May we be found faithful.

My husband was in Australia recently. While there, he was deeply impressed by the writings of George Herbert, a seventeenth-century Anglican priest. Stuart e-mailed one of Herbert's prayers to me that both he and I have used since, to focus our thoughts on the work of repentance as we pray. I recommend it to you.

> *Sum up at night what thou hast done by day,*
> *And in the morning what thou hast to do.*
> *Dress and undress thy soul, mark the decay,*
> *And growth of it, if with thy watch, that too*
> *Be down, then wind up both since we shall be*
> *Most surely judged, make thy accounts agree.*
>
> George Herbert, "The Country Parson"

As we sum up at night what we have done by day and what we have to do in the morning, repairing the altar becomes a habit that leads to a more intimate walk with the Lord.

❧

A PRAYER ABOUT THE WORD OF GOD IN MY LIFE

> *Oh, Word of God, pound on my soul;*
> *drench my life*
> *and make me whole.*
>
> *Accomplish that for which you came;*
> *sprinkle my way*
> *with gentle rain.*
>
> *And if sometimes the Word seems cold,*

help me to read
though it feel old.

For ice and snow can melt with spring,
and in God's time
change everything!

Oh, Word of God, produce in me
a bud, a flower —
who knows? — a tree.

A gentle shade for those in need,
a place where hungry
ones can feed.

A watered garden I would be —
oh, Word of God,
rain thou on me!
Amen.

Discussion or Journal

1. Read 1 Kings 18:16–40. Why did Elijah rebuild the altar of the Lord? What did it represent?
2. What are the building blocks of your Christian life? Fill in the diagram at the top of the following page.
3. Which of these blocks needs repair? Prioritize the first three that need work.
4. Look up and discuss:
    a. Attitude. Philippians 2:5–11. Make a list of the things that characterized Jesus' attitude.
    b. Maturity. Read and think about Hebrews 6:1. Write a sentence about your maturity level in understanding and applying God's Word. What can be done about it?

c. Prayer. What sort of prayer have we been talking about in this chapter? Would you say this aspect of prayer is a priority for you?

d. Church. Discuss or write a paragraph about the following statement: "Church is not somewhere you go; church is something you are".

e. Stewardship. Look up and find out all you can about stewardship from the following verses: Proverbs 22:9; 1 Timothy 3:2–3; 6:3–10; and 1 Peter 5:2.

f. Which of the following building blocks are you keeping in good repair? Share or write down your secret.
   • Holiness
   • Service gift
   • Relationships
   • Growth
   • Trust

g. Read Psalm 92:12–15. Do you struggle with aging? What biblical concept helps you?

Time to Pray

1. Pray about your altar.
2. Pray for your family, friends, and church about their altars.
3. Take time to think quietly about repentance in your prayer life. Talk to the Lord about it.
4. Pray for a spirit of repentance worldwide.

To Do on Your Own

1. Spend time every day this week looking at your altar with God and repairing it.
2. Read the whole of 1 Kings 18 again. Pray about the things you are learning from it.
3. Share the lessons with someone else.

Notes and Ideas

CHAPTER SEVEN

SURRENDER AND FAITH

ALL OF US WANT OUR PRAYERS TO WORK. AS ELIJAH waited for God to send down fire to burn up the sacrifice, so we wait for evidence of God's power to come down upon our lives and ministries. All of us struggle with unanswered prayer, and we are not alone. Elijah was a man "just like us". He must have wondered why Jezebel still ruled the roost in Jezreel when all those prayers were being prayed by the godly few remaining in Israel. He surely had many questions when the widow's little boy fell sick and, despite Elijah's best efforts, died.

All of us wonder what's going on when our prayers are not answered. One reason this may be true, of course, is that our altar lies in ruins. But once we have been alerted to the fact and are putting repentance to work in our spiritual disciplines, we can find ourselves even more confused and disappointed when our prayers still don't seem to produce results.

It could be that we have not truly surrendered to God. Yes, we need to repent, but we need to surrender too. Elijah first rebuilt the altar, which had been in ruins, and then he made the sacrifice.

The bull that Elijah cut up and placed on his altar represented his sin offering to God. The people watching knew exactly what Elijah's evening offering meant. There was one reason for building an altar, and that was to make a sacrifice.

Altars and sacrifices go together. Repentance and surrender go together. Repentance is not complete if we do not surrender to God. And yet we cannot surrender to God if we have not first repaired our ruined relationship with him.

Sometimes we offer God our lives in a prayer of commitment. Yet our altar lies in ruins. "Take my life Lord," we pray fervently. But the Bible says, "If I regard iniquity in my heart, the Lord will not hear" (Ps. 66:18, NKJV). So however fervent our prayer of full surrender may be, God tells us sometimes that we have put the cart before the horse. We need to make sure that the "sorrys" have been said in order that the surrender can be made.

WHAT DOES GOD WANT OF US?

What then does "surrender" look like or, rather, sound like? When it comes time to talk to God about what he wants from us, how should we approach the Lord and what should we say?

Before we do anything else, we need to ask God what he requires for an offering. This is not for us to decide. When you read the Old Testament, particularly the Pentateuch, you are left in no doubt as to what God wants. Whole pages of Scripture are dedicated to spelling out God's requirements in the most minute detail. It would have been unthinkable for an Israelite to offer God a pig or an unclean animal, because they were forbidden sacrifices. Even some clean animals were not allowed for temple offerings because, for God's sovereign reasons, he had designated other animals or birds for such use. Cain got into big trouble because he offered God something God had *not* asked for, and he didn't offer God something he *had* asked for! (Gen. 4:2–17).

Perhaps we kneel down in prayer and offer God an hour of our time on a weekday to help with the youth group. Well, what's wrong with that, you ask? Nothing — if you are responding to what God has asked you to do. But if you have decided that out of the goodness of your heart that is what you can do for God and no more, even though the church needs help in social work or administration, then God will not accept your sacrifice or answer your prayers! Anyway, God does not want us deciding what we will do for him, and when, and where. He wants to tell us what he has in mind.

When you think about it, it's silly to offer God an hour of our time as if it is ours to offer. As David the psalmist observed, our future is in God's hands (Ps. 31:15). All our moments are his, so we should in fact be asking him for an hour of his time to use.

Surrender is an attitude of mind. We need to remind ourselves that everything we have, everything we are, and everything we do is a matter of borrowed time or borrowed resources. It's God's time. Our talents are God's talents on loan to us. Our money is certainly God's money. Our very lives are borrowed. So if we are living on borrowed time, with borrowed lives, exercising borrowed gifts, what we should be asking in our prayers is when God would like for us to do what! We should be praying, "What would you like that is yours today, Lord?" Even our sacrifices are lent to us to give! The bull on Elijah's altar belonged to God first.

Elijah stepped forward on Mount Carmel "at the customary time for offering the evening sacrifice" (1 Kings 18:36). There was a time for each specific offering. I have discovered this principle to be at work in my Christian life. God will tell when it's time for what. All I have to do is do it.

There was a time when he asked me to offer a sacrifice of privacy. Stuart and I met a young girl who needed a home for a time. We were living in very crowded accommodations at the time, and it just didn't seem sensible. After much prayer and reading, we realized that the Bible is full of commands to be sacrificial rather than sensible! More prayer led us to believe that we were right in our convictions. The girl moved in, and our privacy moved out! How could we do this, at this time, in this place? Only by sacrificing some of our privacy. It had to be placed on the altar. We reminded each other that our home was not our own. It was God's. He had every right to invite whomever he wanted to live in it. Is God this specific, you may ask? Yes, I believe he is.

Remember, Elijah was told to offer a bull. He could have made things easy for himself and offered a rabbit instead of a bull. After all, a bull was expensive and a lot of trouble. First he had to find one. Then he had to buy one, and then he had to get it up the mountain. After that he had to kill it and cut it up in pieces. A little animal would have been much more convenient, not as expensive, and a lot less trouble!

But Elijah was working with God to fulfill God's plan. In the hearing of the people, Elijah said to the Lord, in essence, "I have done everything you told me" (see 1 Kings 18:36). When Elijah sacrificed and how Elijah sacrificed was according to God's plan as shown to Elijah through God's Word. God hadn't asked for another sacrifice. So I hope you get the point. All we have to do is what he says, even if we think we have a better idea!

When we respond to God and give him the things he has indicated — through his Word — that he wants from us, there is a certain peace that indicates our sacrifice is acceptable to God.

IS YOUR SACRIFICE ACCEPTABLE?

Immediately the fire of the Lord flashed down from heaven and burned up the young bull, the wood, the stones, and the dust. It even licked up all the water in the ditch! And when the people saw it, they fell on their faces and cried out, "The Lord is God! The Lord is God!" (1 Kings 18:38–39).

When the fire fell on Elijah's sacrifice, there was ample evidence of God's approval. "Something" will happen inside you that will be as definite and obvious as Elijah's fire! It may not be obvious to others, but it will be to you. More often than not you will experience the peace of God that passes understanding (Phil. 4:7). The peace of God is God's kiss. It's his "thank you". It's as if you sense his pleasure at your having offered an acceptable sacrifice. Conversely, there will be no inner sense that God is pleased if you insist on offering him "inadequate" or "convenient" sacrifices.

Over and over in the Old Testament, especially in the writings of the prophets, God stated that Israel was offering him unacceptable sacrifices. One of the best examples of this is found in the prophecy of Malachi.

In Malachi 1:6–14, we read that the people were offering God unacceptable sacrifices. God lets his people know what he thinks about this. He does not mince words. He says they have "cheated" him. The people are indignant, pointing out that they offered the right animals on the right altars. But they had brought flawed gifts — animals that were maimed and imperfect. "Why," God says, in essence, "you would not even give these things to your governor!" Yet the people were offering such gifts to the King! (Mal. 1:6–14).

How often do we offer less than the best to our God? Do we rob him of his just dues? The children of Israel had done just that. Later in Malachi we read, "Will a man rob God?" asks the Lord. "Yet you rob me." "How do we rob you?" the people asked. "In tithes and offerings," the Lord replied (Mal. 3:8, NIV). Even while we pray prayers of surrender, we can cheat and rob God! We offer to God that which costs us nothing, or we withhold from him that which is his by right. Such prayers never get farther than the ceiling.

If our prayers are not getting answered, we should examine our altars and our sacrifices. Are we repairing our altars, and are we placing upon them suitable offerings? What have we placed on the altar of the Lord lately?

What are the sacrifices he requires of us? Have we searched the Scriptures to find out? Have we asked the Lord, "What will you have me to do, to give? Where do you want me to go? Rwanda? Bosnia? Timor? Across the road?" Maybe we dare not ask this for fear that God will want something very close to our hearts. If we dare to really get serious about living a life of surrender, it may well mean that our favorite things get placed on the altar. But if they do, there will be such peace in our hearts that we will kick ourselves for not surrendering sooner!

God may ask you to sacrifice an impure spirit. For some, it is a real sacrifice to give up impurity. Maybe you are in love. Perhaps you are planning to get married. You may even both be Christians. It could be that the devil is telling you that no one needs to know that you are sleeping together. But God knows. And you know and so does the person you love. The angels know, and who knows who else will find out?

God wants you to repair your altar and offer up your impurity. Let it go. Deal with it. Put it where it belongs, on the altar of God. It says in the Bible that we are to keep the temples of our bodies pure. Sexual intimacy is for marriage. The time before marriage, when we're single, is a time set apart for sexual purity. Whatever it costs you to place your impurity on the altar; do it for the Lord's sake, for your loved one's sake, and for your own sake. You will not be sorry.

CAN YOU OFFER PRAISE AS A SACRIFICE?

Sometimes God wants you to sacrifice bad things, and sometimes he wants you to sacrifice good things. Again, it may be that he wants you to give the most precious thing you may possess. Or he may call on you to offer a sacrifice of praise. What is a sacrifice of praise? I've thought a lot about that. I think it means to make a real spiritual effort to praise God in the hard times. Why is that? Because we are all basically very selfish people and the last thing we want to do is to thank God for affliction. The best biblical example of this I know is Job.

Job had a lot to thank God for. He was the richest man on earth. He was healthy, wealthy, and wise. He loved God and God loved him. He acted as a priest and offered up prayers for his family. He was concerned for the welfare of the weak and the poor. This great man had made suitable sacrifices all his life, and God was well pleased with him.

But one day (it had to be a Monday), Job's world caved in. He lost all he had, except his wife and his health. He lost his servants, his wealth, and his children — all ten of them! When the Lord allowed all this trouble to come, Job's wife suggested that he curse God. Why shouldn't he, especially when he had served God so faithfully? Instead, Job got up, tore his robe and "fell to the ground in worship" (Job 1:20, NIV). Then he offered a sacrifice of praise: "Naked I came from my mother's womb," he said, "and naked I will depart. The Lord gave and the Lord has taken away; may the name of the Lord be praised" (Job 1:21, NIV). I can assure you, it took a real spiritual sacrifice for Job to place his rising resentment, bitterness, and anger on the altar and praise God.

A sacrifice of praise does not mean that you praise God for the death of a child or for bankruptcy. It means that, when you can't praise God for what he has allowed, you praise him for who he is despite what he has allowed. Job did not say, "Praise the Lord for allowing my kids to be victims of a tornado, and thank you, Lord, my servants were slaughtered." He was able to thank God for the Lord's sovereign power over life and death.

God was bigger than Job's problem, and "Job did not sin by charging God with wrongdoing" (v. 22, NIV). I assure you that must have cost Job something! We have to give up our desire to charge God with wrongdoing and place our protests on the altar instead. God is well pleased with such sacrifices.

What is God asking you to surrender to him? Perhaps he wants you to sacrifice your complaints about how you think God has treated you and offer him praise instead. When life is not going well, our praise is a costly sacrifice.

Those sacrifices that are unacceptable are the things that are cheap or that cost us nothing. King David wanted to buy the threshing floor of Araunah. The man was delighted to have David ask for it. After all, the king wanted to offer a sacrifice to the Lord on his property. So Araunah offered to give it to the king. David replied, "I will not sacrifice to the Lord my God burnt offerings that cost me nothing" (2 Sam. 24:24, NIV).

I think of all the times I give God things that "cost me nothing". I sit in church and hear an appeal for money or goods for poor people. My hand goes into my purse, and I collect my small change. It feels good to get rid of it. My purse feels lighter, but my spirit feels heavier! How dare I call that an offering. It has cost me nothing at all.

I heard about a young married couple at seminary. They heard an appeal for coats for refugees suffering in a bitter winter. The young couple went into their closet and began going through their clothes. "Maybe this will be a good time to clean out the closet," one of them said to the other. They busied themselves with sorting out the clothes they no longer wanted. Then one of them said, "I feel bad about this. Maybe we should start again." So they began looking at their coats again. Both of them came to the new leather jackets they had been given for Christmas. They stood in silence, looking at each other. "Should we offer to the Lord the coats we don't want anyway, or should we give our best coats?" the man asked his wife. It was hard. They had given up much to study for the ministry. But the outcome was not in doubt — they knew deep and satisfying joy as the coats were taken off the hangers and were soon on the way to Russia, where a poor pastor and his wife cried as they received them. With such sacrifices God is well pleased. Let's not be cheap.

ARE YOU BEING REAL BEFORE GOD?

Not only must we offer acceptable sacrifices but we must be genuine. Let's be real. What do I mean? The Scriptures talk about a show of religious fervor with no substance. This was demonstrated in the life of Israel by the elaborate showmanship in the temple. Feast days were perfect opportunities for people to look religious and act religious, especially when it was time to bring their offerings to the priest in front of everyone else. This was often rank hypocrisy. "These people honor me with their lips, but their hearts are far from me," said the Lord (Matt. 15:8, NIV). Prophet after prophet addressed this problem, but the people continued the big show.

Hosea proclaimed that the Lord wanted people to know that he "desire[s] mercy, not sacrifice, and acknowledgment of God rather than burnt offerings" (Hos. 6:6, NIV). If we merely go through the motions of Christianity and do not live out our faith, even the hours we spend volunteering in the church will count for nothing. If we secretly want to be seen by people, we will have had our reward (see Matt. 6:2).

God is not impressed with our playacting. Once we

stop being cheap and start living sacrificial lives with humble spirits and contrite hearts, then God will be delighted to accept our offerings. When the right time comes for us to make a private or public surrender, we must do it. There is a time for presenting ourselves to God in whatever way he is asking us.

Once I became aware that God was asking me to offer as a sacrifice my time with my husband. I am a pastor's wife, among other things, and that calling requires sacrifice. Some pastors' wives work in the church as hard as their husbands do. I edit a magazine for ministry wives, and a friend of mine wrote an article about her struggle in this area. She talked about the "other woman" in her husband's life — namely, the church! Her husband, she felt, dressed for the other woman, was on time for the other woman, and spent more time with the other woman's children than he spent with hers. Her resentment knew no bounds. However she continued serving the Lord in the church as she had always done. But with these offerings God was not well pleased.

There came a day when she repaired her altar. She knew exactly what the Lord required of her. On her knees in a quiet place, she surrendered to the will of God for her own life and gave God her husband as well. Her life was transformed, and so was her marriage. "All that work I did with that smile on my face, all those hours I spent working my head off in the church counted for nothing because of what was going on inside," she told me. But once she cut up her particular bull and laid it on her altar, the fire fell! Her prayer life was transformed. The effect of that surrender was felt not only in her church but also throughout the whole denomination that she and her husband served. Just as Elijah's sacrifice affected the people, and they acknowledged God and returned to him, so it was in my friend's life. And so it was in my life too.

HAVE YOU OPENED YOUR HANDS?

Sometimes it helps to sit still in the Lord's presence and ask him what needs surrendering. It could be that you don't know what is wrong with you. You may feel far away from God and not know why. Ask him. You may find that he'll show you something you are holding back. When I first came to know the Lord, I used to hear a lot of talk about backsliding. I had a mental picture of a slide and myself on it sliding out of God! But I do not believe you can slide out of God. The Scriptures say "You have died, and your life is hid with Christ in God" (Col. 3:3, RSV). You are secure.

So what does *backsliding* mean? I believe it means "back-holding." It is terribly possible to hold things back from God — things we know we should yield to him. Do you ever feel as if you are clutching something? I know I do. If it is something I should let go of, I go to my prayer place, get still, and let God open my hands. He will pry my fingers, one by one, off that thing or person if I give him permission. As you learn to hold things lightly and not tightly, peace will come. But remember that there is no peace without surrender.

It is a funny thing, but when I think of all the things God has pointed out to me over the years — things I needed to place on the altar — the hardest things to release have not been the bad things but the good things. The blessings of this life can become idols, almost without our knowing it. In fact, so often the only way we become aware that a blessing has become an idol is a lack of peace.

When Stuart and I were raising our children, we immigrated to America. The time came for them to go to college. I found myself facing an empty nest. Not only that, but people began to ask me to speak and write on the subject. I didn't want to, one reason being that I was struggling with it. I had believed that I had "held the children lightly, not tightly", yet I certainly had no peace.

I took some time out to pray about it. "Lord," I complained, "they don't need me anymore." I needed to be needed, and I wasn't! So I sat still a long time until I figured out what was the matter with me. I needed to place my "need to be needed" on the altar. I had to give up my insistence on the kids' dependence on me. The Lord told me I was not giving up my relationship with my young adult children; rather, I was giving up my dependence upon their dependence! Sitting there in that quiet place, I understood why my peace had disappeared. My children had become my idols. A couple of lines of a hymn came to mind:

> The dearest idol I have known,
> Whate're that idol be,
> Help me to tear it from Thy throne,
> And worship only Thee.

Once again I had to repair my altar, then make the sacrifice. Once again the peace came.

Do You Know What to Say?

So what words can we use when the time comes to make our surrender to God? What did Elijah say when he made his sacrifice?

At the customary time for offering the evening sacrifice, Elijah the prophet walked up to the altar and prayed, "O Lord, God of Abraham, Isaac, and Jacob, prove today that you are God in Israel and that I am your servant. Prove that I have done all this at your command. O Lord, answer me! Answer me so these people will know that you, O Lord, are God and that you have brought them back to yourself" (1 Kings 18:36–37).

Well, first Elijah prayed in the name of the one true God — the God of reality, not fantasy, the God of Elijah's forefathers. The nation of Israel had a history with this prayer-answering Deity. Elijah reminded himself that this God he was invoking in prayer was the same God that Abraham had trusted — Abraham, the father of Elijah's faith, who had proved God to be as great as his name. This was the God of Isaac, Abraham's son who, terrified, had watched his father raise the knife over his head to plunge it into his heart, only to hear God's restraining voice from heaven that saved his life. Elijah knew the story by heart — how God had miraculously provided a ram to be offered instead of Isaac, answering both the child's and the father's prayers.

Jacob was part of the story too. Jacob was a man twisted in nature, whom God had transformed from the inside out, changing his name from Jacob to Israel, "Prince with God". Yes, Elijah appealed to the God of his fathers to "do it again!"

Because Elijah prayed in the name of God, he could be bold. So he prayed, "Answer me, answer me." Now that sounds pretty bold to me. There was sureness about this particular prayer that tells me Elijah had gotten things in place in his life. He was praying according to the will of God as revealed in the Word of God. His altar was in good shape. He knew which sacrifice needed to be offered, and he laid hold of the promise of God that encouraged him to pray in faith. He therefore prayed fervently and boldly. He asked God to show everyone just who was in charge in this weary old world of ours. No wonder he prayed with such bold assurance, "Answer me! Answer me!" When as best we know our hearts, and we have fulfilled these conditions as far as sinful imperfect human beings can, then we can go ahead and exercise faith and pray for the fire to fall.

The most important aspect of this whole prayer is the

motivation behind it. Elijah was first and foremost interested in what people did about their faith in God. The reason this was the driving passion of his life was that he cared more about the Lord's heart than his own, more about the Lord's reputation than his own reputation. Listen to the impassioned ending to his prayer: "Answer me! Answer me so these people will know that you, O Lord, are God and that you have brought them back to yourself" (1 Kings 18:37).

When we get around to caring first about God's heart and then about other people caring about God's heart, we will be able to pray prayers of overwhelming confidence. The prayer of faith is not about my demanding outlandish things that occur to my own fertile imagination; the prayer of faith is about my putting things in place spiritually, living a sacrificial lifestyle, and spending my life passionately concerned about God's name. When I boldly pray in this fashion, I will see wonders accomplished. Maybe you would like to use this simple prayer to make the desires of your heart known to God.

❧

A Prayer for God's Power to Fall on Us

Fire on the mountain,
praise in every heart,
altar in position,
people taking part.
Taking on the enemy,
laughing in his face,
showing Israel who is God
of glory and of grace.

Make me an Elijah,
turning men to thee,
giving you pre-eminence,
letting you use me.
When I am discouraged,
touch my downcast soul,
lift my fasting spirit,
sanctify the whole.

May I repair my altar
when tempted oft to doubt
my call to Christian service,
when all I want is out.
I'm trusted with a message
that all may be forgiven;
teach me to pray Elijah's way,
and send down fire from heaven.

So keep me ever faithful,
despite your chastening rod,
to be in tune with purposes
born in the heart of God.
May love for you consume me,
that I may give my all,
and as I make my sacrifice
so let the fire fall.

Let the fire fall,
let the fire fall.
And as I make my sacrifice,
so let the fire fall!
Amen.

Discussion or Journal

1. Which of the following elements of prayer most needs attention in your life?
   • Repentance — repairing the altar
   • Surrender — making an acceptable offering
   • Faith — trusting God for the answer
2. Write a prayer of surrender. Pray it alone or in a group.
3. Make a list from Scripture of some of the sacrifices God requires from all of us.
4. Read Genesis 4:2–17. What was Cain's problem? What is ours?
5. Share or write about a time when God required a sacrifice from you.
6. What are the internal signs of God's hidden approval once you surrender to him?
7. Read Malachi 1:6–14. What does this passage of Scripture say to you?
8. What is a sacrifice of praise?

Time to Pray

1. Ask yourself, *What have I put on the altar lately?* Talk to the Lord about that.
2. Don't be cheap. Be real. Call things by their real names. Do business with God!
3. Use the hymn on page 124 to release something that needs to go to God.
4. Make a sacrifice of praise.
5. Pray these things for others.

To Do on Your Own

1. Develop a sacrificial lifestyle in one area of your life this week.
2. Practice the three aspects of prayer: repentance, surrender, and faith.

Notes and Ideas

CHAPTER EIGHT

THE RAIN MAN

IF ELIJAH HAD A NICKNAME, IT WOULD PERHAPS BE "THE rain man". God used this servant of his to bring back the blessings of the rains that had been withheld from the land because of the people's apostasy.

(Once when Jezebel had tried to kill all the Lord's prophets, Obadiah had hidden one hundred of them in two caves. He had put fifty prophets in each cave and had supplied them with food and water.) Ahab said to Obadiah, "We must check every spring and valley to see if we can find enough grass to save at least some of my horses and mules" (1 Kings 18:4–5).

BEYOND BATTLE TO BLESSING

James tells us that Elijah prayed, and the heavens were sealed, and he prayed again and the heavens were opened (James 5:17–18). God and his servant were working together to show the people of God their wrongdoing and to turn the people's "hearts back to God". The Lord wants all of us to be "rain" men and women, people who learn to have power with God through prayer. We come now to the part of Elijah's story that shows us how he brought those showers of blessing to the thirsty people around him.

Bringing the fire is one thing; bringing the rain is another. Confronting the people of God with their lack of love for the Lord is necessary, but being the agent of blessing is joyful. Praying prayers of blessing is a ministry that brings us a good return, not that that should be the reason we engage in it.

It would have been the easiest thing in the world for Elijah to stop praying when he and God "won" on the mountain. But he was able to rise above his natural desires and get his people back, and he began co-operating with the Lord of life in the work of blessing.

You see, God's plan goes beyond judgment and confrontation. His goal is always to renew us. He had to be harsh — allowing the years of drought — to bring people to a point of desperation and honesty. Once the people came face-to-face with God's power and the necessity to choose life with God or death with Baal, the Lord was ready to send the rain and renew them.

Just as renewal was God's plan for his people back then, it continues to be God's plan for the church today. It appears that God has ordained special periods of blessing for his people. Just as he brings new life and fruitfulness through the natural seasons, so he wants us to know a spiritual spring and summer in our lives and service. There can be no life without rain, and God is the ultimate Rain Man.

God pours out his Spirit like life-giving water. A number of Scripture passages convey this message: "I will pour water on the thirsty land, and streams on the dry ground; I will pour out my Spirit on your offspring, and my blessing on your descendants" (Isa. 43:3, NIV; see also Isa. 32:15; Ezek. 39:29; Joel 2:28–29; Acts 2:17–18). But the Holy Spirit is not only poured into us, his children: He wants to pour himself out through our lives like streams of living water, bringing blessing to others.

The people of Israel had to die first — die to their selfishness, sin, and idolatry. Israel had begun the work of repentance at Carmel, and now a new day had dawned and Elijah was determined to be a big part of it. Will we do this work? Will you and I become godly, allowing God to do his renewing and refreshing work through us? Will we be rain men and rain women? Don't miss out on this wonderful prayer work. It's the best! Many of us, however, take a break when it comes to praying for revival. Perhaps we are spent. We should follow Elijah's example.

Think about it. This man had just had one of the best days of his life. Up on top of the mountain he had shown everybody what God could do in answer to prayer. The power of God had been seen in the most dramatic fashion. A whole nation had rejected Baal and turned back to God. Consider all that happened: An entire nation converted to God in one meeting; the wicked king of Israel finally did what a man of God told him to do; Jezebel's prophets got dispatched to their just deserts; and Elijah himself was able to call the shots according to the Lord's will. I think that such a day must rate in anyone's book as a spiritual red-letter day.

The prophet could have been forgiven if he had decided he had done his bit and that it was time to take it easy. But Elijah was wise enough to hold the ground he had taken from the enemy and keep praying for refreshment and renewal. In fact, he'd only just begun. This was the first day of the rest of his life. Now he was vindicated in the eyes of the people. *Today,* Elijah perhaps thought, *today will be the day I go back to Jezreel and be established as a prophet of the Lord. But first, I must pray for rain.* So he climbed to the top of the mountain and got down to work. This was the climax of three years of divine planning, and Elijah could hear the strangest sound. It was a sound only he and God could hear; it was the sound of an abundance of rain! (1 Kings 18:41).

I want to hear what God hears, don't you? God wants

all of us to be so in touch with him that we are tuned into heaven's wishes for earth. Remember that Elijah was "a man just like us", and we, too, can "hear" what God has in mind and pray prayers that work as effectively as Elijah's did if we have a mind to.

There are showers of blessing that God has planned for the human race. He has his prescribed way of releasing them, and his methods haven't changed. Do you know any folks with lives that are dry and cracked? Parched people desperate for a refreshing of heart, mind, and spirit? I do. And I want to do more than preach to them. I very much want to be an instrument of help and blessing in God's hands. I want to be the bringer of good news. It is not enough to have fire on my mountain and be established in other people's eyes as some spiritually important person; I want to be more. I want to be the agent of revival and blessing for my world.

BEYOND THE FOOTHILLS TO THE MOUNTAIN

When I look at Elijah's story, I see things I can copy. Things I can do. First I need to climb high enough.

> Elijah said to Ahab, "Go, eat and drink, for there is the sound of a heavy rain." So Ahab went off to eat and drink, but Elijah climbed to the top of Carmel (1 Kings 18:41–42, NIV).

It doesn't surprise me that Ahab went off to eat and drink instead of climbing the mountain with Elijah! But before we get too critical of him, we should look within. If we are being honest, perhaps we might cry, "Oh, my 'Ahab' heart!" Like Ahab, so often I go off to eat and drink rather than climb to the top of the mountain. And if my conscience gets the better of me and I do set off for the climb, I find myself quitting in the foothills!

I have never thought of myself as a quitter. I look at the hard work I do and ask, "What more do you want of me, Lord?" And I clearly hear him answer, *It is what I want* for *you, not what I want* of *you that matters*. He is not a slave driver. He wants us to be co-laborers with him. We are not God's hired hands.

In John's Gospel, Jesus told his disciples that he was not a hired hand:

> The hired hand is not the shepherd who owns the sheep. So when he sees the wolf coming, he abandons the sheep and runs away. Then the wolf attacks the flock and scatters it. The man runs away because he is a hired hand and cares nothing for the sheep (John 10:12–13, NIV).

In effect, Jesus said, "Nobody hired me." The Father did not look around heaven and say, "What is it going to cost me in hard cash or reward to get one of you angels to go down to that obdurate human race and sort them out?"

Jesus and the Father already had a plan of love for us. When Jesus left heaven to come and seek and save that which was lost, he could hear the sound of blessing to come, the sound of a great rain. He came to pay the price, not to get paid, because he loved us. He had been on the mountain of God and had seen the rain cloud coming, and that's what he wanted for you and for me.

Do we consider ourselves hired hands of God? If so, then we will quit before we get to the top of the mountain. How much more fulfilling to care for others as Jesus cares for all of us and to climb to the top of the mountain out of the persistence that springs from love. God is not going to twist our arm to get us up that mountain to be part of this plan of blessing. But he wants us to join him on the mountain, primarily for our sake, not his.

But we won't see the blessing of God if we don't climb high enough. Hanging around the foothills of faith brings no reward, and even stopping halfway up for a breather won't give us enough of a heavenly perspective. So let's not be quitters. Many of us work our heads off for God, but when it comes to the prayer mountain, we are quitters. One reason for this could be that we are not expecting the climb to be so strenuous.

Would you count yourself a quitter where prayer is concerned? What is your excuse? Are you a "foothills of faith" person? Or are your excuses more earthbound? "I'm too old," you say, or, "I'm too young." "I could be feeding the hungry, healing the hurting, planning an evangelistic campaign, or strategizing with experts about reaching the unreached. I should be writing books, answering e-mail, watching TV, or playing tennis." Elijah could have had all the excuses in the world to quit after Carmel, but he set his face to go up the mountain to pray. So let's climb high enough.

Think of Jesus. He climbed his mountain called Calvary, and he didn't quit. A poster in a young boy's room caught my attention. A football player sat disconsolately on the bench. He had obviously had a very bad game. The large caption across the top of the picture read I QUIT. At the bottom of the poster were the words I DIDN'T! Across them was the shadow of a cross. Jesus didn't quit praying for us, and he didn't quit dying for us when the mountain got high and the way got rugged. He just kept climbing. Will we? Will we just keep climbing?

Not long ago I was aware that a circumstance in my life was getting out of hand. In the past, much prayer had gone into this particular situation, and some of the problems had been resolved. So I quit praying about it. I quit halfway up the mountain. Oh, I didn't stop altogether, but once God had begun to resolve some of the issues, I reasoned that I could coast. The devil, of course, fueled this idea and encouraged me to let up. Once things got out of hand again, I realized what I had done. I happened to be writing this particular chapter at the time! Kneeling down at the side of my bed in a hotel room, I repented in tears. Then I packed up my tent and set off up the mountain again. Don't camp on the hillside; head for the top.

BEYOND POSTURE TO ATTITUDE

Once we arrive at the peak, we will do well to follow Elijah's lead. Having taken the effort to climb high enough, he then bent low enough to be effective in his prayer work. Bending down to the ground and putting his face between his knees, he began to pray. He couldn't get any lower than he was.

Posture is only important if it mirrors what is going on inside of us. It matters nothing to God if we raise our hands to heaven, fall flat on our faces before him, or kneel in seeming penitence with our faces to the rising sun if our hearts are not right with God. In Elijah's case, his posture mirrored his attitude. He was using every part of himself to pray. Elijah used all of himself — his body, mind, and spirit — as he prepared to do his work. So prayer posture is not as important as what it represents. In essence, Elijah was saying, "Lord, I couldn't get lower before you than this!"

Years ago I was working with our church youth, producing a play. We were taking it on the road in an attempt to reach kids outside of the church. One of the young people in the cast was acting up and needed reprimanding about some inappropriate behavior. The next time our group ventured out, we were praying together, and I heard the young man's voice, muffled and almost inaudible. I looked up in surprise to see him flat on his face. His prayer went something like this. "Oh, Lord, I can't get lower before you than this. Forgive me for my foolishness. Thank you for giving me a second chance. Amen!" That young man was using all of himself to pray. His posture reflected his heart, and God appreciated that. So did I! We should take a good reflective look at our prayer or worship and ask ourselves, *Does my body truly reflect my heart? Or am I just posturing?* If we are merely posturing, then that needs to be dealt with before we can be a source of blessing to others.

My husband was speaking at a missionary conference. He noticed a young woman who looked decidedly unhappy. At the end of the service, my husband asked those who wished to, to kneel and pray. The young lady did so. *That young lady is kneeling down on the outside, but she's standing up on the inside,* my husband said to himself. He was right. It turned out that she did have serious attitude problems. Among other things, she didn't want to be on that particular mission field in the first place.

Posturing in prayer will show eventually. You just can't keep up the effort. God of course sees the play-acting immediately. Conversely, he notes sincerity of heart and rewards it. Honesty, humility, and helplessness form the basis of effective prayer. God looks at the posture of my soul. If he sees my soul on its knees, he will reward me. A sense of spiritual poverty is what God is after. Jesus said, "Blessed are the poor in spirit" (Matt. 5:3, NIV). He did not mean those who are "poor spirited", but rather the "happy humble", who make voluntary humility a holy habit. But how do we achieve this voluntary humility? We should dare to ask the Lord to keep us humble! That is a prayer he will always answer.

So just what in my life is hindering the refreshing of the Lord? If you are at all sincere and really don't know, he might tell you if you ask him. You can pray, "Why have you withheld the rain, Lord?" He might not tell you until you have done some serious soul searching. Look into your past and see if there has been some breakdown in your prayer disciplines. See if there are any broken promises to repent of. Once you realize where you failed, be quick to acknowledge it. It might even be helpful to record your repentance in a book.

BEYOND LONELINESS TO PARTNERSHIP

The next thing that the prophet shows us is the usefulness of human help in this spiritual work. Elijah did not go up the mountain alone. He took someone with him. A servant appears in the story. We are not told who he is and where he came from, but he is there. He has come to pray. He has come to help, to watch God work his miracle of grace.

Such help is invaluable. Who do you take up the mountain with you? Who of your friends, family, or colleagues are willing to climb high enough and bend low enough with you? "Where do you expect me to find such a prayer friend?" you may ask. Maybe you feel too shy to invite someone to share your burdens. You may think that most people have trouble enough of their own without taking on any more! But you are not asking them to simply add to their burdens; you are inviting them to participate in carrying the burdens of the Lord! You will find that this makes a difference.

I'm glad that we are not told the servant's name. It is my experience that such companions are usually unknown, unsung heroes. Perhaps they are unknown to the world at large, but they are certainly known and loved by God. They are invaluable members of the Lord's prayer troops. As Aaron and Hur held Moses' arms steady in the battle against

Amalek (Exod. 17:12), so this unknown servant warrior of the Lord strengthened Elijah's arms.

Many such servants have blessed me in my own life. One particular "heart partner" was instrumental in keeping me up my prayer mountain for years. Together we pioneered a work among unchurched children, and the battles we went through were fought together on our knees. Sometimes she watched and I prayed, and sometimes I watched and she prayed. How encouraged we both were by the other. Ask God to give you a "heart partner" to watch for the rain cloud with you. It's hard to quit if someone is right there with you. Incidentally, one such friend will do. It's nice to have more, but start with one, and don't be waiting for more recruits for the army before you commence the battle.

BEYOND PRAYING TO WATCHING FOR ANSWERS

Then he said to his servant, "Go and look out toward the sea."

The servant went and looked, but he returned to Elijah and said, "I didn't see anything." Seven times Elijah told him to go and look, and seven times he went. Finally the seventh time, his servant told him, "I saw a little cloud about the size of a hand rising from the sea."

Then Elijah shouted, "Hurry to Ahab and tell him, 'Climb into your chariot and go back home. If you don't hurry, the rain will stop you!'" (1 Kings 18:43–44).

So first climb high enough, and then bend low enough. Try to take along a friend to watch and pray with you. After that — persist. We climb high enough, we bend low enough, and then we pray long enough. Having arrived at the top of the

mountain, Elijah settled in for the long haul. He was determined to wait until the rain came. He persisted. He didn't
quit. He kept sending his servant to look for the blessing. The
servant looked and looked, but there was nothing. Can we
keep going when there is nothing, until there is something?
Six times the servant came back, saying there was nothing,
but that didn't faze Elijah for a minute! He persevered.

When Jesus was asked how many times we should forgive someone, he replied, "Seventy times seven" (Matt.
18:22, NKJV). This was a phrase in his time that meant ad
infinitum. In other words, "Don't count, just go on forgiving." So in the same vein, don't count, just pray! Persist.
When you know that what you want is what God wants, you
can find strength to persist. You can go on going on until
you see a small token of hope on the dark horizon. The
question we can ask ourselves is not Can I, but Will I?

But what do I do when the rain is so long in coming?
Sometimes you take a turn watching, and sometimes you
take a turn praying. Watching and waiting make up the hardest part of prayer sometimes. The "waiting room" is always
difficult, especially for people brought up in an "instant" society. When it's time to be in God's waiting room, take plenty
of reading material with you. Take your Bible or a helpful
Christian book. Or spend time thinking about the Lord's past
mercies and all the times before when he has sent the rain.

Remember Past Experience

I find it especially helpful to think of some experiences in the
past that God has turned around for me. I go over them bit
by bit, reminding myself how dark and hopeless it all seemed
and then of the way God moved in turning the whole thing
around. I let myself savor the memory of those incidents and
then simply pray, "Do it again, Lord, do it again!"

"Do it again prayers" are a great way to go when you

get discouraged. Once I was impatiently waiting for the raindrops to fall for a family member. It was a case of praying for conversion. In this instance, I began to doubt that God would "do it again". So I spent some time lying on my bed reliving my own conversion experience. I came from a background similar to that of the person I was praying for. As I thought about it, I marveled at the way I had been prayed for with such persistence. I also marveled at the perfect timing of the events leading up to my conversion. After I had revisited that experience, I found myself praying "do it again" prayers with renewed confidence. As we persistently remember the mercies of God from the past, we will find it easier to persist in the present.

Pray for Endurance

Most of us quit before the rain comes, but we should pray about quitting before we actually do it. If you find yourself about to quit, stop right there and say, "Lord, I am just about to stop praying because I am very discouraged. I see nothing at all in answer to all the praying I've done already. There is not a cloud in the sky, and so I am about to give up. If you want me to continue, please give me some help; give me some hope." I have found that when I pray like this about quitting, I don't! Somehow help comes, and I put my head down and go on. So if you are having trouble persisting, first remember past mercies, and then pray for endurance. After that, make it a habit to scan the horizon.

Scan the Horizon

Start looking earnestly for the rain cloud. Look around the whole situation until you see a tiny answer to prayer. Just a little cloud, no bigger than a man's hand. Sometimes we get discouraged because we don't think anything is happening unless there is a storm-swept sky. We need to learn to discern the approach of the blessing that God will surely send our way. Look for the little things before the big things appear.

When Florence Nightingale went to the Crimean War with her heroic band of nurses, she believed with all her heart that God was sending them there. But when they finally arrived after a horrendous journey, the officer in charge tried to send them away. The soldiers didn't want women around in that ghastly environment. The nurses were confused and begged to stay and help, but the soldiers were adamant. This was no place for women, they said. The nurses prayed hard. It had been incredibly difficult to get there. And they had been so very sure God had sent them.

After a week or so, during which the camp commander refused to let the nurses do one thing, Florence went to him and begged him to at least let them scrub the filthy floor of the makeshift hospital. He relented, but said, "Only the floor now, and then you have to go home."

So the nurses rejoiced and got to work scrubbing the floor till it was spotless. They saw God's hand in this "small" answer to their prayers. They felt like Elijah's servant on the top of Carmel. They had seen a tiny cloud on the horizon, and they believed God for the rest. Sure enough, within a few days the camp commander allowed them to do another job and then another, until the sky became black with clouds and the rain finally came. These great women of God learned to scan the horizon for the smallest sign that the Lord was at work, and seeing that "small" cloud, they took courage to believe that God's full answer was on the way.

What is God asking you to pray for? Have you become discouraged by how few signs there are of his answer? Look up, scan the horizon. Watch for the little answers, and take heart. Soon the sky will be full of the evidence that God hears and answers prayer.

For example, your child may hate going to church. You

have been praying for a change of heart. And now you are discouraged. You have been expecting him to say, "Mom, I really can't wait till Sunday so I can go to church! And, Mom, I've decided I want to be a pastor when I grow up!" After all, you have been praying hard about it. But think a bit. Didn't you pass his room the other night and see him kneeling by his bed saying his prayers? And that without you telling him? There you are — it's the rain cloud! Maybe it's no bigger than a man's hand, but it is on the horizon, and it is there to encourage you not to quit but to pray on for the showers.

It could be that you have been praying for someone you work with. The one who is giving you a hard time about your faith. Perhaps you are tempted to give up. After all, she has not brought her Bible to work to read during lunch. She has not been ordering a missionary magazine so that she can learn about missions! Look up. Scan the horizon. Didn't you hear her tell someone that she watched Billy Graham on television the other night? And she said that what he said made sense. It's not much. It's not a huge cumulus cloud, but it's a start. Pray on now for the rest.

Enjoy the Rewards

It helps to realize that there are rewards to waiting. "Really," you say. "Like what?" The first reward is that you mature. "But I don't want to mature," you wail. "It's too painful!" It's more painful to be stunted in your spiritual growth, and anyway, you'll appreciate the blessing all the more if you have had to wait for it.

Another thing waiting means is that you learn lessons to pass on to others. Do you know anyone who is looking for a rain cloud? Someone who could use a break? Anyone who has had too many bad breaks and has almost given up hope? They are just the sort of people who need you. Come alongside them. Share your story with them. Put on your spiritual climbing boots, and climb the mountain with them. Encourage them to hang in there. Watch the horizon. Insist on believing God is a God of the impossible. Declare it loudly and clearly so that doubt flees. Sit in the "waiting room" with them for as long as it takes until the little cloud appears. Then it will be worth the wait; you'll see. Then you will enjoy the rewards of waiting together.

After the waiting was over, Elijah came down the mountain and told Ahab to get going back to Jezreel before the rains stopped him. Presumably, the king was procrastinating. The thought of his wife waiting up for him to talk about the murder of her beloved prophets was probably enough to keep him eating and drinking forever (particularly the latter!). But Ahab, impressed as he was with Elijah's "in" with the Almighty, complied.

> Meanwhile, the sky grew black with clouds, the wind rose, a heavy rain came on and Ahab rode off to Jezreel. The power of the Lord came upon Elijah and, tucking his cloak into his belt, he ran ahead of Ahab all the way to Jezreel (1 Kings 18:45–46, NIV).

What a fabulous climax to the story. Can't you just see Elijah, long legs flashing, his hair flying in the wind, as he raced in front of Ahab's chariot? The rain would catch them now, but it must have been an absolute joy to be drenched with the saving liquid. Exulting in God's long awaited blessing, the two men raced on.

You may ask how Elijah could do this. Where did he find the strength? The answer is in the text. "The power of the Lord came upon Elijah and... he ran" (1 Kings 18:46, NIV). Ah, so that was it. After the season of intense prayer, God bestowed the power to run even in front of a horse and chariot! God promises to all who do his work that they will have the power of the Lord. Not power for just the work of prophet and preacher but for the work of prayer as well.

In the book of Acts it says that after Jesus' disciples had a season of prayer (brought on by the threats of their opponents), the place where they were meeting was shaken, and the Holy Spirit fell on all who were there (Acts 2:1–4). Those who were there that day were ordinary men and women just like you and me. They had access to the same power that you and I have access to. Is this exciting, or what? Are you thirsty for the refreshing of the Lord? Will you climb the mountain? Will you climb high enough, and will you bend low enough, and will you persist until revival comes? If so, there will be enough power to go around to accomplish the work of God for our land, and the refreshing will come.

∽

A PRAYER ABOUT UNANSWERED PRAYER

> *Tender Jesus,*
> *caring for the ones who care not anymore —*
> *for those beaten by circumstances*
> *and driven by sorrow*
> *to believe that they are lower than dogs,*
> *bereft of a reason to live —*
> *hear our prayers.*
>
> *Tender Jesus,*
> *moved with compassion for the sorrowing —*
> *teach us the work of prayer.*
>
> *Tender Jesus,*

[handwritten:] Father we thank you for the tenderness of the Saviour. Moved with compassion for the consequences of sin the sadness and the sorrowing. the weariness of the sacrifice. heavy hearted His sufferings. We thank you for His actions on behalf intervention of those of us the lost and without hope in the world.

145

teach us the perseverance of prayer
in the face of a silent heaven
when you ask us to wait a while
for the answers to our petitions.
See us —
those who would see you smile
and feel your hand of blessing.
Touch awake faith in a Father who cares:
a Father who will never reject,
who is active on our behalf.
Oh, Lord, teach us the patience of unanswered prayer!
Amen.

Discussion or Journal

1. Contrast Ahab's and Elijah's reactions to the events on Mount Carmel. What does this tell you about each of them?
2. Do you agree with the idea that "if you haven't climbed high enough and you haven't bent low enough, you won't see the rain cloud"? Can you think of any other verses that support this concept?
3. Where are you on your way to the summit? On the foothills of faith? Halfway up? Enjoying the view from the top? How can you move on to the next stage?
4. Do you have a "servant" — a heart partner in prayer? If not, where would be a likely place to find one?
5. Which posture of prayer helps you and why?
6. Share a story about how God brought something out of nothing in response to prayer.
7. What are the rewards of waiting?

Time to Pray

1. Pray for all the believers you know who live in the foothills of faith.

2. Pray for the quitters. Pray for persistence.
3. Pray for countries that need a shower of blessing.
4. Pray God will use you to bring refreshment to spiritually thirsty people.
5. Pray for a heart partner or partners.
6. Pray for the Ahabs of this world.

To Do on Your Own
1. In preparation for the next chapter read 1 Kings 19:1–9.
2. Think of someone you have quit praying for. Start up again.

Notes and Ideas

CHAPTER NINE

RUNNING OUT OF PRAYERS

———————— ❧ ————————

HAVE YOU EVER RUN OUT OF PRAYERS? I'M SURE YOU have. Where and when did you experience your low point? Was it after failure or success? We can understand our prayer life being affected when we are in trouble, but what about it being affected by achievement?

We left Elijah running to Jezreel, toward victory and acclamation, toward a career as a distinguished prophet of the Lord. God had vindicated him by fire. But suddenly Elijah turns and runs in the opposite direction.

> When Ahab got home, he told Jezebel what Elijah had done and that he had slaughtered the prophets of Baal. So Jezebel sent this message to Elijah: "May the gods also kill me if by this time tomorrow I have failed to take your life like those whom you killed."
>
> Elijah was afraid and fled for his life. He went to Beersheba, a town in Judah, and he left his servant there. Then he went on alone into the desert, traveling all day. He sat down under a solitary broom tree and prayed that he might die. "I have had enough, Lord," he said. "Take my life, for I am no better than my ancestors" (1 Kings 19:1–4).

Elijah runs away from Jezreel, from fame and fortune, and into the jaws of defeat. The contrast is incredible. But James reminds us, "Elijah was a man just like us" (James 5:17, NIV). He had his highs, and he had his lows. He was just like us, human and afraid. Yes, he was afraid! (1 Kings 19:3).

This particular verse of Scripture is an amazing verse. I could imagine the Bible saying that Elijah was exhausted or Elijah was angry or Elijah was lonely, but not "Elijah was afraid!" Yet, I have to admit that that particular verse of Scripture encourages me to keep hoping, because I, too, am so often afraid.

What do we do when we run out of faith and run into fear? Do we end up like Elijah, flat on our faces under the proverbial broom tree? (v. 4). How do we react when Jezebel's messenger stops us in our tracks?

After Ahab arrived home, he "told Jezebel everything Elijah had done and how he had killed all the prophets with the sword" (1 Kings 19:1, NIV). Needless to say Jezebel was not impressed! In fact, she soon sent Elijah a succinct message: "May the gods deal with me, be it ever so severely, if by this time tomorrow I do not make your life like that of one of them" (19:2, NIV). The Bible then says simply and without comment, "Elijah was afraid" (19:3)!

It has been my experience that when you run into fear you can run out of faith in a hurry. Fear paralyzes you. I have always been a fearful person. When I was a small child, I feared I wouldn't ever grow up to be a big child. When to my surprise I did grow up, I feared I would never live long enough to get married. When I got married, I was frightened I would never have children. When I had three, I spent a fair amount of time worrying that they would fall into the washing machine and drown! When they made it safely past the years when that unlikely event was possible, I worried that they would never get married and have children. And so on and so forth.

I am very familiar with the fear that chases faith away

and leads to a failure of nerve. And it can all happen in a moment! In a moment you can go from faith to fear and end up under a broom tree wanting to die. But such failure is never final for the people of God. It might look final and it might feel final, as I'm sure it did to Elijah, but as we shall see, this fear would lead to a whole new dimension of ministry and experience in prayer.

WHAT FEAR DOES TO FAITH

Stuart and I live in Wisconsin, where it gets very cold in the winter. In fact, snow and ice are a big part of our lives during the long winter months. Sometimes we get a blizzard. It is almost impossible to drive in these conditions. You can be inching along, and all of a sudden you run into what is called a "whiteout". You literally go blind for a moment and become disoriented as the snow swirls around the windshield.

We can experience whiteouts in our faith life too; the blizzards of life can catch us unaware. We could call these experiences whiteouts or "doubt outs." You can see perfectly clearly one moment, and the next moment you are disoriented and blinded by the storm. Doubt does that to you. Doubt is faith in distress, and it is very hard to pray when you are doubting God. The Bible says, "Anyone who wants to come to him must believe that there is a God and that he rewards those who sincerely seek him" (Heb. 11:6). Elijah was experiencing a mammoth "doubt out". He couldn't see God anymore, but worse, he could see Jezebel very clearly indeed. And Jezebel looked so much bigger than God. It's funny what things people are afraid of, isn't it? Here is Elijah, who has taken on an entire nation, running away from a woman! But then, doubt and exhaustion do strange things to you. It's easy to lose perspective.

There are two ways of looking at a problem. You can

look at your problem through God, or you can look at God through your problem. If God is in front of the problem, the problem appears to be insignificant. But if God is behind the problem, then the problem dominates everything.

When we lived in the English countryside, I was alone with the children for a long period of time while Stuart was away, and we were overrun with field mice. I wasn't a bit bothered about going out on the streets and contacting wild teens, but I panicked about the mice! They bothered me especially when I was under a lot of stress. It really is funny what people are fearful about. But whether the problem is as big as Jezebel or as small as a mouse, you need to look at it through God, who is bigger than everything!

What God's Presence Does for Us

The first thing to do when you arrive under the broom tree is to quit everything. That's right, give yourself permission to collapse. Elijah didn't pretend or remonstrate; he didn't sulk or pout. He simply said, "God, I've had it!" Elijah was experiencing serious burnout: "I have had enough, Lord" (1 Kings 19:4). Listen to him, and then be encouraged to be this honest yourself when your turn comes. God wants us to say whatever we want to say. He doesn't care what we say as long as we keep talking. "Talk to me," he says. "Yell if you want, you won't faze me."

Think of the parent dealing with a child who is thoroughly upset. There is nothing worse than being subjected to the silent treatment. If only we can get the child talking, we can do something toward resolving the issue. God feels like that about his children. It is not that he needs information, just dialogue. It is for our sake, not his, that we should try to tell him exactly how we feel.

The Lord Jesus never tired of inventing, encouraging, prompting, exhorting, even commanding people — especially his disciples — to pray. He said that they "should always pray and not give up" (Luke 18:1, NIV). But when you are under the broom tree, that is very hard to do; it's hard to even believe he hears us. It's hard to come to him "just as I am", isn't it? Something inside of us tells us that we have to be in a right frame of mind before we talk to God. How then can we tell God that we have "had it"?

If we are talking about intercession, then, yes, we must believe that God is a rewarder of "those who sincerely seek him". But here we are not talking about intercession. When you're under the broom tree, your prayers are not intercessory prayers but rather prayers of desperation. We are thinking about the dark night of the soul, when we can't hang onto our faith any longer. Yet Hallesby encourages us to pray on, even when we are driving through a blizzard of unbelief! He says,

> Many have had most remarkable answers to prayer when they had no clear or definite assurance that they would be heard, either before they prayed, while praying, or after they prayed. It has seemed to them that God has given the most remarkable answers to prayers at times when they had no faith whatsoever!

So keep talking to the Lord even if you are mad at him or doubting his very existence.

Where was God in Elijah's situation? God was right there in the person of the angel of the Lord.

> Then he lay down and slept under the broom tree. But as he was sleeping, an angel touched him and told him, "Get up and eat!" He looked around and saw some bread baked on hot stones and a jar of water! So he ate and drank and lay down again.

Then the angel of the Lord came again and touched him and said, "Get up and eat some more, for there is a long journey ahead of you" (1 Kings 19:5–7).

God himself is always present and waiting to help his exhausted servants. Jesus promised that a sparrow would never fall without the Father knowing it. Note, he never promised that a sparrow would not fall, but he did promise the sparrow would not fall without the Father's knowledge of it. God is never surprised by our visits to the broom tree. In fact, he meets us there and cooks us breakfast! Knowing all things, he waits to strengthen us by the appropriate means.

Who is this angel who baked the loaves and provided the jar of water? None other than God himself. The Angel of the Lord is called different things in different parts of the Scripture: the Angel of his Presence, the Angel of the Covenant, or the Captain of the Lord of Hosts. This is one of those places where God manifests himself as an angel and where the person he appears to is immediately aware of who he is. Elijah addresses him with familiarity. He knows that the angel is God indeed.

Who wouldn't want an opportunity to talk to the Angel of the Lord of Hosts? Imagine being face-to-face with God. Yet every time you and I pray, he, the Angel of his Presence, is as much with us as he was with Elijah! He is the precious Angel of the Lord to us in the person of the Holy Spirit. In fact, he dwells within us. We take him with us under every broom tree we visit!

So let's see what happened to the humbled prophet under his trauma tree. What were the reasons Elijah found himself there? What caused him to doubt God? What brought him to this, his lowest point?

God Deals with Our Stress

Elijah had been under sustained pressure for a very long time. When we live with stress, with no letup, we can find ourselves at the end of our resources. Physical exhaustion can affect us emotionally, psychologically, and spiritually. Perhaps you have had the experience of nursing an elderly parent through a long and terrible illness. Then your marriage falls apart. Add to this, a visit to the doctor that thoroughly frightens you. Then a storm causes flash flooding on your property, and on top of this you lose your job. Is it any wonder you are seen heading for the broom tree? Life with its trials can sap us. And so can life in the church.

If we are doing anything right, we will be tired in the Lord's work. Have you noticed how few willing hands and hearts there are to serve? But there is a difference between being tired in the work of the Lord and being tired of it. My husband says he was born tired, he has lived tired, and he expects to die tired! There are never enough hands to the work. However, he says, if he gets to heaven and he is still tired, he is coming straight back! The tiredness that Elijah was experiencing was not ordinary tiredness, the "weariness in well doing" that the Bible speaks of (see Gal. 6:9). Elijah's problem was rather a spiritual weariness that was a far more serious thing.

Different people react to stress in different ways. It was not just that Elijah was a "worn-out prophet". Elijah's personality could have helped to take him down and keep him down. I have the sense that Elijah was an intense sort of man, a perfectionist, an overachiever. He probably expected an enormous amount from himself. Our strengths are often our weaknesses. Maybe you can't stand to do anything badly. You find it difficult to take on anything unless you excel at it. You feel a need to do it better than anyone else has ever done it before.

It could be that you remarried after a divorce. You inherited children, and you have some of your own too. You are determined to be Super Stepmom! But of course you can't fulfill your own expectations — nobody can. Like Elijah, you throw yourself down on the ground and cry, "Take my life, for I am no better than my ancestors" (1 Kings 19:4). It's hard coming to grips with your own personality, especially if you can't stand to fail. It takes courage to accept the way God put you together and deal with your perfectionistic tendencies. It's galling for the overachiever to know that no one who came before him did all of it right, and he won't do all of it right either! But he won't do all of it wrong. Some of it will be wrong, but not all of it. Remember that we are fallen, so at best we can only be the best, fallen Super Stepmom, or the best Christian servant we can be.

It sounds as if Elijah was comparing himself with his forebears and was coming to terms with this very thing. He was feeling that he had failed just as they had failed. He wanted to be better than his ancestors, because, I suspect, Elijah wanted to be better than everybody, and when he found out he was just like everyone else, he couldn't take it. "'Lord,' he said, 'Take my life, for I am no better than my ancestors'" (1 Kings 19:4). When you become desperately disappointed with yourself, it can land you flat on your face, like Elijah. But that is often an ideal place to begin to lower your own expectations of yourself and get a more realistic view of life.

The Bible talks about us taking a good look into the perfect law of liberty. It speaks about seeing a true picture of ourselves there. It says we should then go away wiser, live with what we have learned, and make the changes that we have seen are necessary. "For if you just listen and don't obey, it is like looking at your face in a mirror but doing nothing to improve your appearance. You see yourself, walk away, and forget what you look like" (James 1:23–24).

This reminds me of a time I was caring for my three-month-old grandson. The only way I could keep him quiet was to jiggle him up and down in front of the mirror. "Look" I said to my daughter. "He sees himself in the mirror."

"No, he doesn't," my daughter informed me confidently. "Babies that age think that's another baby!" I accepted her knowledgeable statement, child development being her field, and thought about her words.

So often I behave like my grandson. I am reading the Bible and come across a wonderful bit of advice and think at once of whom it pertains to. *Why*, I say to myself, *this is ideal for so-and-so.* I see another baby in the mirror!

Perhaps Elijah had been seeing other babies in the mirror for a long time. He had been thinking about what needed doing in the lives of his fellow Israelites and had forgotten that he was "no better than his ancestors". Well, now he was seeing his own reflection clearly in the mirror.

Some of us do better with the stress of life and ministry than others. It is tied up very much with our personalities. As we have said, if you are an overachiever like Elijah, your great strength could also be your great weakness. Some of us never feel we work hard enough, pray long enough, or know half enough. And maybe we fear that we'll never live long enough to listen to our bodies and learn to live within our limits. Take our physical well-being, for instance. Elijah types don't usually look after themselves very well. It's interesting that the first thing God did was to see to Elijah's physical needs. God himself cooked the prophet breakfast!

What a practical thing to do. When somebody is down, do something really practical, like taking a meal round to the broom tree. Try looking after the children so a hassled single parent can get away for a break. One of the things Stuart and

I try to put on our calendars is a time each year when we move into our busy children's lives and look after their kids for three days or so, just to let them get away on their own. We like to think it contributes to their sanity and, therefore, to our grandchildren's well-being!

The Lord can deal with the pressure in our lives, whether it comes from our circumstances or from our self imposed expectations. The broom tree exposes these pressures for what they are.

God Deals with Our Loneliness

Another way we arrive under the broom tree is that we have been isolated for too long. Loneliness drives you to the broom tree. Elijah had had his share of isolation, and maybe you have too. You may have had to move time after time, and this has led to isolation. There has never been enough time to make close friends. Or you might have been transferred abroad for your job, and you are really lonely for someone, anyone, to speak your own language.

Things can get out of perspective if you withdraw from fellowship or are forced to stop going to church. Even the life of a young mother can isolate you if you are home all day shut up with the company of small children. Being isolated for whatever reason can cause you to lose your perspective. Any one of these elements that Elijah experienced would have brought a person down, but Elijah experienced all of them at once.

God Deals with Our Exhaustion

The first thing God did for his tired servant was to tell him to go to sleep. Sometimes when I used to get really spent, I believed I should fall to my knees in prayer and read the Bible until I dropped. But now when those times come, I know the Lord is saying, "Go to sleep, Jill, we'll talk in the morning!" Would the Lord ever say, "Put your Bible away"? He has said that to me. Those of us who are intense need lots of permission to let down before we collapse altogether.

Help yourself by building in suitable breaks when you really relax. All of us relax in different ways. Some of us have to put "Have fun" on our calendar or it doesn't happen. And some of us relax by doing nothing at all, while others of us find relief by changing our activity. I am in the latter group. It causes a whole lot more stress for me to lie in a deck chair or lounge on the beach than to do something entirely different, like gardening or bird-watching. We need to find ways to help ourselves, and we won't do that unless we know ourselves well enough to build some suitable valves into our lives to let the pressure off. Stop. Boundaries are not unbiblical. Here we have God encouraging Elijah to relax and look after his body.

"But there's so much to do and so few doing it," we wail, rather like Elijah, who kept reminding God that he felt like he was the only one doing anything. That's what we usually feel like when we lose perspective, but actually all that is irrelevant. We are not supposed to be doing the work of all the people who aren't doing their part, although a certain amount of that is inevitable. We are supposed to be listening to the prompting of the Holy Spirit, who will prompt us to stop doing any work when we are really pushing it. The Holy Spirit acts like a prompter in a play. When it's time to come off the stage, we should do it. If the other actors are falling down on the job, that's not our problem. If we get off track, the Spirit will surely cue us. But he only prompts us to do our part and not everybody else's.

We are body, soul, and spirit, and all three belong to God. All three must be taken into consideration, and God does that. If it is a physical need, he will address it, as he did here. I can't imagine what the food the Angel of the Lord provided for his servant tasted like! But just the fact he cooked it for him must have been enough for Elijah.

Years ago I was traveling in the Deep South of America. I had been on the road continually and had missed meals along the way. I had also missed planes and trains, and my schedule was thoroughly messed up, as was my body. Arriving late at a camp, I made my way to the kitchen to see if I could find some food. But the room was all locked up, and there was no one around. Sitting there hungry and tired at the midnight hour, I prayed a rather silly prayer. "Oh, Lord, I would love a peach!" It was just what I craved at that moment. I gave up and went to my room. There on the doorstep was not one peach but a whole basket of peaches! I had no way of finding out who put them there. But it was as if the Lord said to me, "The journey is too great for you — have a peach, Jill!" You have no idea how that little act of kindness lifted my spirits. It was as if the Angel of the Lord cooked me breakfast that day.

The journey can get too great for all of us, for all sorts of reasons. Maybe we have been left to care for a sick person for far too long with no relief. Or we have been in school and also working to support a family and have burned out. Maybe we have been in a wilderness situation spiritually, with little or no fellowship over the long haul; yet others have expected us to give out continually. Perhaps we have become despondent dealing with past issues, or we are fearful about a grim future. It may be we are living or working with a difficult person who is sapping us emotionally, or we are dealing with teenagers who are giving us a run for our money. There are all sorts of reasons the space under the broom tree is limited these days. Whatever the problem, however, Jesus is "the same yesterday, today, and forever" (Heb. 13:8). It was the Lord Jesus, the Captain of the Lord of hosts, who came to Elijah's aid, and the same Captain of our salvation will fight for us against all our enemies, even the enemies called desperation and depression.

God Deals with Our Disappointment

I find that when I'm checking into the Broom Tree Inn, I lose my perspective of God. All I can think about is how disappointed God must be with me. I envision the Lord standing over me with a big stick with *ministry* written on it. I become convinced that he is telling me to get my act together and share the Four Spiritual Laws with Jezebel! Yes, it's easy to lose your perspective.

I have to remind myself that I can never surprise God. Why, the bread was hot on the stones by the time Elijah arrived on the scene. In fact, all that God expects from us is failure of one kind or another along our spiritual road. The good news is, he waits around the corner of our failure with the teapot boiling, the bread hot upon the stones, and our bed ready with turned down covers! He has a plan — a plan of renewal and refreshment — and he waits at the reception desk of Broom Tree Inn, ready and eager to check us in! What we need to do is co-operate. We should lie down and sleep. We should get up and eat. Then we should lie down and sleep again (1 Kings 19:5–7).

Whatever medicine God the Healer prescribes, we should take it. And we should rest long enough for the loving treatment to take effect. Elijah waited until he was strong enough to go on before he went on. Then, "strengthened by that food, he traveled forty days and forty nights until he reached Horeb, the mountain of God" (1 Kings 19:8, NIV).

What brought you to this point? Was it a church that hurt you or a spouse that abandoned you, or did you abandon a spouse? Maybe you are under the broom tree because of things you cannot change. Perhaps you are the victim of a cruel circumstance. Wrong choices that others made have had severe consequences for you. Perhaps, like Elijah, you are mostly disappointed with yourself. When you haven't lived up to your own high standards, it is only a matter of time before you decide that God can do without you and so can everyone else!

I can remember getting into that state of mind only once. I was under a lot of stress, with my husband out of town and my father sick with cancer. Things were not going well in the youth work I was responsible for, and then our daughter fell off a donkey and broke her arm. Stuart was in America making plans for us to immigrate at the time. I was supposed to be wrapping up the work we were responsible for and packing up the house.

One day I couldn't ignore the gnawing pain in my stomach anymore, so I went to the doctor. He told me I was suffering from an ulcer, and he put me in the hospital. Suffering from a great imagination as well as a bleeding ulcer, I was quite sure that I was going to die and that this would be a lot better for all concerned. God would give Stuart an American wife who could do the job in the States a whole lot better than I could, and everyone would bene-fit. It sounds funny now, but it wasn't funny then. It was awful.

As I meet pastors' and missionaries' wives in my work, I often hear similar stories: "My husband would be better off with another wife," some tell me. And they mean it. That's a broom tree feeling! It is a horrible place to find yourself. As I think back to how the Lord lifted me out of my deep despondency, I realize that God may have allowed me to go through it so I could encourage others. Looking back I can see that my experience was not unlike Elijah's.

The Lord put me in the hospital, and I had a complete checkup. Not that Elijah had that luxury, but the first thing both of us received was physical help. If you are in this predicament, have yourself checked out. It isn't unspiritual to look after your body. People helped me practically, and I had to learn to let them. God brought Elijah breakfast; friends brought my family supper!

And then I found lots of help in the Word about God's great concern for me. "The journey is too great for you," I read over and over again. God was not mad at me for being in the state I was in; he was loving and caring and infinitely patient. Above all, I became convinced that God was not finished with me yet. Failure is never final.

God "touched" his servant Elijah at the lowest point of his life, and God touched me as well. He didn't do it in quite the same way, but he touched me nevertheless, and I continued on my way, strengthened by the nourishment he provided through the Bible, Christian friends, and above all, prayer. God will find a way to touch you if you give him a chance to minister grace to you.

WHAT THE BROOM TREE EXPERIENCE GIVES TO US

The broom tree experiences in our lives introduce us to a new way of praying. It's not verbal praying but rather a total abandonment of ourselves in despair at God's feet. It is a wordless praying, a silent scream for help. Sometimes we cannot even shout at God. We are spent.

When you run out of prayers, God can still hear you! Even though no words are formed or spoken, God looks at you and reads the language of your longing. At that moment, you see, you are the prayer! So be content to just be a desperate prayer under your particular broom tree, and wait and see what happens!

You may wonder how long you will be there. You'll remain there as long as it takes for you to be strengthened. Try not to take on anything extra until things begin to be resolved. Once Elijah was off and running again, God went ahead of him, preparing his future. That is definitely what happened to me.

Stuart said that I had to stay put in England until I was well enough to face the immigration process, and I gradually regained my health and began to pack for the journey to the States. God went ahead of me every step of the way.

How will you know God has touched you and that it is time to move on? You will know if you sense God's love and acceptance. You will feel this sense of inner well-being far deeper than at the emotional level. The Holy Spirit does not come into our hearts to do his deepest work in the shallowest part of us. He works his healing grace at the mind level first. Once you hear him saying something kind and sweet, believe it, get up from under your broom tree and go on to Horeb, the mountain of God.

If Elijah had not believed that "God was not finished with him yet", he would have died of a broken heart under the broom tree. If I had not believed that I was redeemable, I would have tried to persuade my husband to stay home and not immigrate to America. As I lay miserably alone in that hospital bed, I remember giving a desperate glance heavenward. It was all I could manage, but it was enough. *I am a prayer, Lord,* I said without words. *Read me.* Words are nice, but words are not needed when you are under the broom tree. Just be content to know that every word you would have said, if you could have said it, is heard loud and clear among the angels and by the Lord. God hears you. His ears are especially tuned to those sorts of prayers — to the solitary, silent scream!

So where does this leave our hero? Sadder and wiser, certainly. Elijah came to terms with his humanity and with his fallen humanity at that. The expert on the subject of prayer learned that there are some times when you run out. You run out of faith, out of energy, out of friends, and out of hope. You run out of the human resources to function anymore. You run out of belief, and you run out of ideas, and you even run out of prayers. When that happens, God has only just begun! As Elijah was to find out, God gives more grace, more help, more joy, more hope, and more strength to all of us in our weakness than he ever does when we are strong. We just need to bank on it.

> *He giveth more grace when the burden grows greater;*
> *He sendeth more strength when the labors increase.*
> *To added affliction He addeth His mercy;*
> *To multiplied trials, His multiplied peace.*
>
> Annie Johnson Flint

❧

A Prayer for Those Who Are Despondent

> *Dawn in my darkness,*
> *deep in my heart,*
> *tell all the shadows*
> *to swiftly depart.*
> *Send out your love light,*
> *dispelling despair;*
> *dawn in my darkness,*
> *tell me you're there!*
>
> *Dawn in the drabness*
> *of dreary days,*
> *color my life*
> *with perpetual praise.*
> *Paint with your paintbrush*
> *a heavenly view;*
> *dawn in my darkness,*
> *tell me it's you!*

Dawn in my darkness,
bring me new hope,
wake up my spirit,
help me to cope.
Use me to tell others
just who you are:
"My Dayspring, my Sunrise,
my bright Morning Star!"
Amen.

Discussion or Journal

1. Have you ever had a broom tree experience? What took you there? Can you identify with any of the factors that took Elijah down? Have you ever run away because you were afraid?
2. Do you find it hard to tell God how you feel? Have you ever told God you've had enough?
3. Who was the angel of the Lord to you? Look up Genesis 16:7 and Exodus 3:1–16, and discuss other incidents when he appeared. Ask.
   • What was the occasion?
   • To whom did he appear?
   • What did he do?
   • What was the result?

Time to Pray

1. Pray for people under the broom tree.
2. Pray for yourself, during your own broom-tree time. Ask God to help you look at your own pressures, loneliness, and exhaustion.
3. Make a list of practical things you could do to help someone like Elijah. Pray about it, then go ahead and act!
4. Spend some quiet moments "being a prayer".

To Do on Your Own

1. Read 1 Kings 19:8–18.
2. Do you know anyone under the broom tree who needs your help? Make a list of three things you can do for him or her. Then take action.

Notes and Ideas

CHAPTER TEN

THE STILL SMALL VOICE

WHATEVER THE LORD PUT INTO THE BREAD THE DAY he fed Elijah under the broom tree, kept Elijah going for forty days and forty nights until he arrived at Horeb (Mt. Sinai), the mountain of God.

> So he got up and ate and drank, and the food gave him enough strength to travel forty days and forty nights to Mount Sinai, the mountain of God. There he came to a cave, where he spent the night (1 Kings 19:8–9).

Now this was a very special mountain. It was referred to as "the mountain of God" because so many incredible things had happened there. Moses, who was a fugitive at the time, had met the angel of the Lord near this place (see Exod. 3:1–4) and had been called to bring the children of Israel out of Egypt and bondage (v. 10).

It was at Horeb that God had given Moses the Ten Commandments (see Exod. 24:12), and it was at Horeb that Moses had broken the stone tablets they were written on (see Exod. 32:19–20)! Here Israel had made the Lord angry at their idolatry, yet it was in this same place that he forgave them and sent them on their way (see Deut. 1:6; 9:8). It was at the mountain of God that water had come miraculously out of a rock when the people were dying of thirst (see Exod. 17:6), and it was there the Israelites repented and stripped off their ornaments to show God they were sorry for their sin (see Exod. 33:6). This was quite a mountain, and it is easy to see why Elijah headed for it.

REVISIT YOUR ROOTS

When you are in trouble, where do you run? If it is possible, I run back to my roots, and I think that's what Elijah did. When things have gone wrong, I think of someone I know who has guided me in the past, and I try to get in touch with that person or call him or her on the phone. I want to go "home" and see the stable people who brought me up or visit with an old friend who has helped me before. Or sometimes, when I'm really in turmoil, I just have an almost unbearable yearning for my mother!

If you ask me why Elijah ran to Horeb, then I would tell you that I think he wanted to get back to his spiritual roots. And that is a good idea. When you are strung out and don't know which way is up, revisit the foundations of your faith. What do you know about God — really know? What do you believe deep down about his character? What do you remember of his dealings with people, in love and grace? Go back to the roots of your religion, as long as it is orthodox Christianity.

Elijah got settled into a cozy cave and began to think. All that had happened in that mountain in the past must have seemed part of the very air he breathed. History has a way of reminding you of the omnipotence, omniscience, and omnipresence of God. And that is good when you feel you have no power, know nothing, and cannot be in all the places you want to be at once!

Perhaps Elijah spent time rehearsing the momentous events that had occurred on those slopes. Which bush had burned with the fire of God? Which rock was the one that gave Israel that life-giving water? Where had Moses seen the face of the Lord? How must it have been to watch the finger of God write the Ten Commandments on two pieces of rock? Perhaps Elijah began to pray again on the mountain. Did he — at first tentatively, and then with increasing boldness — begin to talk to God again? Or did he wonder where God was? Did he shout and scream and cry out in frustration? We don't know.

When I was in South Africa in 1999, I heard a phrase that well describes someone's behavior at these times. Speaking of a grown man — a politician who was at the end of his tether — a friend said, "He was so frustrated he started to throw all his toys out of the crib!" Very descriptive! Have you ever felt like that? I certainly have. If I haven't actually resorted to such infantile behavior, I have wanted to!

It looks as though Elijah had been on the mountain only one night before the Lord said to him, "What are you doing here, Elijah?" (1 Kings 19:9). He recognized it at once, of course.

> Elijah replied, "I have zealously served the Lord God Almighty. But the people of Israel have broken their covenant with you, torn down your altars, and killed every one of your prophets. I alone am left, and now they are trying to kill me, too" (1 Kings 19:10).

I can hear Elijah thinking, *What does he think I am doing here? He knows they are after my hide. Doesn't he want me to be safe? After all, I have zealously served him.* God was thoroughly aware of Elijah's fervent service and all his efforts on God's behalf. But he wanted Elijah in the right place, which may or may not always be the safest one. Elijah was in the wrong place, and that was the issue, not whether he was safe or not. God knew there could never be peace of mind outside the will of God for a child of God.

"Go out and stand before me on the mountain," the Lord told him. And as Elijah stood there, the Lord passed by, and a mighty windstorm hit the mountain. It was such a terrible blast that the rocks were torn loose, but the Lord was not in the wind. After the wind there was an earthquake, but the Lord was not in the earthquake. And after the earthquake there was a fire, but the Lord was not in the fire. And after the fire there was the sound of a gentle whisper. When Elijah heard it, he wrapped his face in his cloak and went out and stood at the entrance of the cave.

And a voice said, "What are you doing here, Elijah?" (1 Kings 19:11–13).

Suddenly there was a great storm. God was approaching. His footfall split the rocks and caused the earth to quake. There was a hint of his nearness in the mighty wind that sprang up. God was drawing near. His appearance to Elijah was heralded by fire on the mountain, just as his aura had appeared to Moses long ago. By now Elijah was familiar with God's footfall, and he waited with his heart beating hard, wondering if God was coming in judgment. But when the storm was over, he realized God was not in the wind but rather in the whisper of mercy and grace that followed it. God does not always do things in a big way. His genius can be seen in the snowflake as clearly as in the blizzard, in the raindrop as well as in the cloud.

I can't help but wonder if the Lord wanted to heal and renew Elijah under the broom tree, and Elijah ran away. He was certainly off course by the time he arrived at the mountain. But you cannot outrun God! See how infinitely patient and forgiving God is with Elijah. God is the great forgiver and restorer of our souls. Bank on it, because, however bad you feel you have let him down, he is already working to bring forgiveness and new life. So remember, the next time you find yourself running off course, that the Lord has no intention of letting you run right on out of his will and purpose. Try as you might to run out, God will give you your waking thought, and it will probably be "What are you doing here, Elijah?" Have you noticed how piercing and insistent that "still small voice" is?

I know a man who ran the race of faith well and then ended up under a broom tree. He had been a great teacher of the Word, but then stopped reading it altogether. Instead, he gave himself over to sport. He raised horses and involved himself in the party set. He told me that there wasn't a day that went by when he didn't have to work at chloroforming his conscience. Scripture that he had learned as a child hurried after him even as he tried to hurry away from it. Every moment, every day, he heard that "still small voice" asking him, "What are you doing here, Elijah?" In the end, he stopped running and started kneeling instead and as a result was wonderfully restored to the Lord. The voice may come to us in a quiet whisper, as it did to Elijah and to my friend, but it will be the most insistent whisper you have ever heard! Thank God for it. He loves you far too much to leave you out of his will and purpose for your life.

So maybe a trip back to Horeb is necessary for you in your state of heart and mind, but don't expect God to leave you there for long or give up on you even if you have given up on God. Listen to the whispers of his grace. Revisit your past, and then renew your disciplines. "Go out and stand on the mountain in the presence of the Lord" (1 Kings 19:11, NIV). Once more Elijah put himself intentionally into the Lord's presence. Then he waited. The holy habits of his previous days needed to be re-established. "Go and stand," the Lord commanded him, and Elijah did so.

Can you hear the Lord's still small whisper in your heart? What is he saying? Well, go on, just do what he is telling you to do. Put this book down for a bit, and listen for God instead of listening to me! How happy I would be if you began to read his words again right now instead of mine. Re-establishing contact starts with stopping everything and listening for the once familiar whisper of God.

Once you hear God's voice, answer him. Try to respond to what you know he is saying to you. In Elijah's case, God kept at it until the prophet heard him, really heard him. Eventually Elijah came to terms with the fact he was not supposed to be here, he was supposed to be there! Do whatever it takes to stay on the mountain in the presence of the Lord until you know where you are meant to be. Stay still until you get an inkling of divine direction. When you have dealt with your past and come to terms with your present, then you will be ready to take on your future. "So Elijah went from there" (1 Kings 19:19, NIV).

But how do we know the whisper is God's whisper? How can we be sure that Satan is not whispering in our ear? That's a good question. We know that Satan does speak thoughts into our minds, and if he can appear as an angel of light, he can also sound like one. There are a few things we can do to recognize his voice.

First, ask yourself, "Does this thought fit with Scripture?" God does not whisper thoughts into our minds that contradict his written Word. That's why we should get familiar with his Word as soon as possible. Before my husband went into ministry, he worked for a British bank as a bank inspector. His job was to catch white-collar criminals who got their money mixed up with the bank's money. His training was simple. The young trainees were put in a room with piles and piles of pound notes. Among the thousands of bank notes that were genuine currency were a few counterfeit ones. The idea was simple. It was presumed, correctly, that if you counted masses of real money, you would immediately recognize counterfeit money. If we continually read Scripture, we will instantly recognize the voice of error.

Second, ask, "Does this thought talk about the will of God, the glory of God, or the name of God? Does it honor him?" In Elijah's case, God kept reminding him that the people needed to glorify God. If the things you are hearing are not complimentary to the person of the Almighty, you have a right to question who is talking to you.

Third, ask, "Does the thought accuse me or excuse me?" Satan is "the Accuser... who accused our brothers and sisters before our God day and night" (Rev. 12:10). "Brothers and sisters" means you and me. If I am hearing condemnation, I should question who is whispering in my ear! The Lord may rebuke you, but he won't condemn you, so listen carefully to what you are hearing. And the Lord won't excuse you either. He will confront you with the necessary words and lead you back onto the right track. When Satan talked to Eve in the Garden of Eden, he excused her for being disobedient. God will never do that. Rather he will call us to repentance. Satan will never do that! God is intent on whispering us back to obedience, so ask yourself if what you are hearing in your head is leading you to obedience.

See what God said to Elijah: "Go back the way you came" (1 Kings 19:15). In other words, when his servant was ready and God had dealt with the fear factor, the fatigue factor, and the forgiveness factor, he issued some pretty straightforward commands. He sent Elijah back the way he had come, and Elijah found himself back in tune with the mind of God. By retracing his steps, Elijah got back to where he belonged.

RECOGNIZE THAT OTHERS ARE WITH YOU

And where did Elijah belong? Spiritually, he needed to be free from his gripes and grudges. He had been whining that he was the "only one left". He had been feeling that he was the only one in Israel who was spiritual. "These Israelites are an uncommitted lot," he complained bitterly to the Lord. Sometimes we get to feel a bit like that, don't we?

It could be you think you are the only spiritual one at church. You are the first to volunteer and the last to leave the premises because you are conscientious. No one turns up at the prayer meeting except you, and no one offers hospitality to the missionaries except you, and you are fed up with the unresponsive people around you.

Well, maybe you need to take note of the Lord's words to Elijah: "Yet I reserve seven thousand in Israel — all whose knees have not bowed down to Baal and all whose mouths have not kissed him" (1 Kings 19:18, NIV). Fortunately we are responsible only for our own response, not other people's, and we can't know people's hearts anyway. Instead of working on our grudges, we should work on God's grace in our own lives. When we look after our own business and let God deal with his, we enjoy the fruits of his faithfulness instead of getting frustrated.

God wants us to use the pain he allows so that it will drive us to himself. Elijah was hurt, lonely, and bitter. People had treated him unfairly; more than that, they were trying to kill him. When bitter things happen to you, don't let your enemies win. The people had almost killed Elijah's faith, and his very life was threatened. Now he had to decide if he would allow them to kill his ministry too. He decided not to give them that satisfaction.

Tough things happen in ministry. Churches have been known to finish off their pastors. One of the most extreme examples of this came to our attention in the course of soliciting articles for our magazine for ministry wives and women in leadership, *Just Between Us*. The special section that month was on stress. Al's story won the prize! This man knew firsthand how Elijah must have felt.

While Al was pastoring a growing church, a church split erupted that literally tore the church apart and destroyed Al's family. (His wife divorced him and died shortly afterward.) "There was one woman who caused the church to split," he said. "She tried to get everyone out of that church that wasn't either from that town or related to her. It took her almost two years, but she did it." The conflict eventually claimed Al's ministry and the life of a deacon who ended up committing suicide. A lawsuit came out of it, and a man attempted to stab Al to death inside a church full of people on a Sunday morning, but a member of the church saved him. And you think you have problems!

Like Elijah, Al headed for the bushes, and for several years he wandered alone in his pain. His friends and colleagues had deserted him. But God was faithful. He began speaking to Al and asking him what he was doing. Then God began to drop wounded pastors who had had similar experiences on Al's doorstep. (These were like the seven thousand who had not bowed the knee to Baal.)

Realizing he wasn't alone, and not wanting other pastors to feel the abandonment he had felt, Al dealt with his bitterness and resentment, and God sent him "back down the mountain" again to begin Restored Ministries. There are hundreds of people today who have received healing and renewal through the ministry of this man and his new wife as they go about the country at the invitation of congregations in trouble. Al didn't waste his pain. When the whispers of God's grace came to him, Al listened and obeyed the Lord's command to "go back the way he came".

One day, while in my own pain, I wrote this poem:

Don't waste the pain; let it prove thee,
Don't stop the tears; let them cleanse thee.
Rest, cease the striving; soon you'll be arriving in his arms.
Don't waste the pain — let it drive thee deeper into God.
He's waiting, and you should have come sooner.

I pray that you will come sooner than I did and that God will help you use the pain to help others.

So, the Scripture says, Elijah left Mt. Sinai (1 Kings 19:19). He left Horeb with a spring in his step and a plan of action. First he had to retrace his steps, for God had told him, "Go back the way you came" (v. 15). We, too, may have to retrace our steps before we can move forward. Pastor Al had to retrace his steps and attend to some unfinished business before new ministry began.

Ask the Lord what he wants you to do, whom he wants you to talk to, and when he wants it done. Look at the specific instructions that God gave to Elijah (1 Kings 19:15–19). Once you are back on track, there will be no doubting the action that needs to be taken. God will give you specific things to do.

Relinquish Your Grip on Your Ministry

He replied again, "I have zealously served the Lord God Almighty. But the people of Israel have broken their covenant with you, torn down your altars, and killed every one of your prophets. I alone am left, and now they are trying to kill me, too."

Then the Lord told him, "Go back the way you came, and travel to the wilderness of Damascus. When you arrive there, anoint Hazael to be king of Aram. Then anoint Jehu son of Nimshi to be king of Israel, and anoint Elisha son of Shaphat from Abel-meholah to replace you as my prophet" (1 Kings 19:14–16).

One thing Elijah had to do was political, one thing was national, and one was personal. Living as God's person in God's world will require our involvement in every echelon of society. But the thing that intrigues me is the personal part of the plan. It was time to pass on the baton. I wonder what Elijah thought when the Lord said, "Anoint Elisha son of Shaphat…to succeed you as prophet" (1 Kings 19:16, NIV). Maybe he thought, *But I've only just begun!* Or perhaps he was hurt and wanted to argue with God about his choice of a successor. Maybe he would have liked to have had some input on the matter.

One thing that is interesting is that God chose Elisha as surely as he chose Elijah. It had been settled before the foundation of the world. When we wonder who should be doing what, it is a very good idea to ask the Lord! Much prayer should bathe the process to make sure that God's will is done and that the right person is in the right place.

In the New Testament church, when a new apostle was chosen to replace Judas, it was not left up to a few to decide. Peter stood up among the believers (Acts 1:15), a group numbering about 120, and said: "'May another take [Judas's] place of leadership'" (v. 20, NIV). "Then they prayed, 'Lord, you know everyone's heart. Show us which of these two you have chosen to take over this apostolic ministry'" (Acts 1:24–25, NIV).

How much prayer goes into choosing leaders? Do we rely on C.V.s or on corporate prayer? Do we pray first or last? You can be sure that Elijah's choice was birthed in prayer. While God was talking to his servant in the cave, he made it abundantly clear whom Elijah must anoint as his successor.

Whether or not Elijah found it difficult to let go of his

own ministry, he obeyed God and went to find Elisha. This was the man who was to wear Elijah's mantle. Elisha would carry on Elijah's work, but first Elisha would have to learn many things from his mentor.

Mentoring is quite popular in the church at the moment. (I think mentoring is just another name for discipleship.) Anyway, Elijah set about training his successor for the ministry ahead. Elisha appeared to be up for the challenge. He asked for permission to say goodbye to his family, burned his bridges — or, rather, his plows — behind him, and set off to serve Elijah. I like the way the Bible puts it: "Then he set out to follow Elijah and became his attendant" (1 Kings 19:21, NIV).

It was a privilege to wear someone's mantle, especially someone as famous as Elijah. But remember that we know Elijah as the hero we've read about. To the people in Elisha's world, Elijah's role was not so clear-cut. We can only surmise that something had been going on in Elisha's heart to have prepared him for this call.

When it was time for my husband and me to come to the church in America, I could feel God preparing me to leave one ministry and go to another. At the very same time, my best friend began to feel that change was in the air for her also. We began to pray together about it. Then we involved others in prayer. Slowly and surely, I felt God calling me to cast my mantle on Angela's shoulders. As I lost my burden for the work I'd been involved with in England, Angela gained a burden for it. Before, she had been my assistant. But as we prayed over all this, we switched roles, and I became her assistant. It wasn't hard. I saw that God had given Angela a double portion of the blessing he had given me, and the transfer was soon complete. Thirty years later, she is still in leadership in that work.

I have found this to be a pattern. Those with whom I

have shared the yoke in ministry testify to the same experience. We must all learn to pass on the mantle when the time comes. It is tempting to hang on to a position we have worked for, but if God says to cast the cloak, we had better be obedient. When the time came to move on to ministry outside my local church, the Lord told me to let go of the women's ministry I was responsible for. God had been preparing a young and godly woman to be my Elisha. "She's too young," some said. "She's too inexperienced," said others. "She doesn't have children," objected another. "How can she relate to young mothers?" All this may have been valid if we had been talking about a secular position. But this was ministry, where different criteria pertained.

"How do you know you have the best possible person for the job," a leader asked me, "if you don't interview lots of candidates? We must be sure we have the very best!"

"It's not a question of the very best, qualified person," I replied. "It's a question of finding the right person." The right person might not appear to be the "best qualified" but the most qualified person in the world will not be able to do the job if he or she is not the right person!

So how do we find the right person? How did Elijah?

So Elijah went and found Elisha son of Shaphat plowing a field with a team of oxen. There were eleven teams of oxen ahead of him, and he was plowing with the twelfth team. Elijah went over to him and threw his cloak across his shoulders and walked away again. Elisha left the oxen standing there, ran after Elijah, and said to him, "First let me go and kiss my father and mother goodbye, and then I will go with you!"

Elijah replied, "Go on back! But consider what I have done to you."

Elisha then returned to his oxen, killed them, and

used the wood from the plow to build a fire to roast their flesh. He passed around the meat to the other plowmen, and they all ate. Then he went with Elijah as his assistant (1 Kings 19:19–21).

Pray for Guidance

It was as Elijah and God talked alone in the cave that God told him who was his "right" person to succeed him. I'm sure the choice of Elisha raised eyebrows around Israel. Why hadn't Elijah chosen one of the professors at the schools of the prophets? Why hadn't Elijah done "a proper job search"? I can hear Elijah telling his critics, "God told me whose shoulders must carry my mantle. He chooses who will serve him, when, and where. It was God himself who indicated just who would take my place." Next time your committee is searching for a person to take over an essential ministry, resist the temptation to fill the vacancy with merely a warm body, and start to pray until God shows you who your Elisha is.

Allow the New Leader to Do the Job

Once you have called "Elisha", the next thing you will have to learn to do is let the person do things his or her own way. Let the person make mistakes. After all, you did. Elijah made mistakes, and because he hadn't always done things right, he probably made allowances for Elisha's mistakes. I remember a young pastor on our staff thanking my husband for giving him the freedom to fail. "I made plenty of mistakes when I was learning," my husband responded, "so that helps me to let you make them too!" Do we give people we work with that freedom? Try not to give people responsibility without authority. That's not fair. But once you have given them that authority, make sure you give them the freedom to use it and to make their mistakes.

Elijah made it abundantly clear to Elisha that he was to

be in charge, but he also made it clear to the students in his Bible schools just who was going to be taking over. When the time came for Elijah to go to heaven, the prophet made sure the students witnessed his exodus and the obvious transference of power to the younger man (2 Kings 2:11, 15). You can help the transition of power by affirming the "candidate" in people's eyes. Be generous in your remarks, and build the other up in conversation. There is really a lot "Elijah" can do to help a young Elisha.

As far as we are concerned, we should always be alert to the still small voice of the Lord telling us when to step down. We are not to be building our own empires but rather God's kingdom. If we are not sure about the details, we should wait on God until we are sure. Half the problem with church ministry is that we have managed to get too many square pegs in too many round holes. We rush to fill positions and end up choosing people God has not chosen. If we spent more time praying, God would help us get it right.

Elijah didn't appear to find it hard to let go. When the time came to leave, Elijah told Elisha and prepared the younger prophet for his exodus. Are you finding it difficult to let go of a cherished position at church? Maybe you have built a good Bible study, and the idea of handing off the leadership is painful for you. Dare to pray that you won't stay on one moment longer than you should. The results of staying too long could prove disastrous for everybody.

RECEIVE THE MANTLE WELL WHEN IT'S GIVEN TO YOU

As we turn our attention to Elisha for the rest of this book, we will see what an excellent job Elijah did in training his successor. If we want to see our work remain, we must pass on the mantle at the right time and in the right way. It will be the fervent prayers of righteous men and women that accomplish this.

But perhaps the situation is turned around, and the mantle is being passed to us. Let's learn from Elisha's example how to receive mentoring.

Elisha was minding his own business when Elijah appeared in the field where he was working. Elisha was plowing with the last team of oxen (1 Kings 19:19). Not too many people saw what Elijah did to Elisha. This was a quiet summons, but a summons Elisha was prepared for. He asked if he could say goodbye to his family, a request that was granted. He then gave a feast for his plowmen, chopping up his plowing equipment to make the fire to cook the meat. He literally "burned his bridges" behind him. He knew that that's what it was going to take to accept Elijah's mantle. Just as in marriage, there will need to be a leaving of the old life as we take up the new, so in ministry there needs to be a leaving and a cleaving as well. We must burn our plows in order to give ourselves fully to the next task the Lord has for us.

Once you have reordered your priorities to accommodate whatever it is God is asking of you, then, like Elisha, you will need to begin with a willingness to learn all you can from your mentor. A teachable spirit is of great price in the eyes of the Master. Elisha became Elijah's assistant (1 Kings 19:21), serving in whatever capacity Elijah asked him to. Good followers became good leaders. Do we know how to assist? Do we know how to be humble and to submit to leadership? Then we will make good leaders when our turn comes.

And do we know how to love those who lead us? It appears that there was genuine affection between the two men. Read the account of their last day on earth together, and see how Elisha's loyalty comes through. He refused to leave his teacher, even though Elijah gave him every opportunity (2 Kings 2:1–12).

Do we know how to be loyal? Loyalty is a great virtue and one that can make a team strong. When conflicts arise, do we refuse to talk about our leaders behind their backs, but rather go to them in person and talk things through? Somehow I cannot imagine these two biblical colleagues backbiting!

And do we know how to pray together as we do the work of the Lord? I can imagine that, being such a man of prayer, Elijah prayed a lot with his young assistant. It is praying together that will bind us together. It is as we seek the face of God and the will of God that we shall see the fire of God in our joint ministries. One person praying is good; two people praying is better. Jesus said, "Where two or three come together in my name, there am I with them" (Matt. 18:20, NIV). There is power in having a prayer partner. And those of us privileged to experience this can testify not only to the blessing in our own lives but, more important, the blessing in the work of the kingdom.

It was nearly time for the transfer of power to take place. I'm sure Elisha didn't feel he knew enough, was prepared enough, or could do enough to make a difference in his world. But he knew what to ask for. He knew that without the Spirit of the living God he would be totally inadequate to carry on the work. And so he asked Elijah, "Let me inherit a double portion of your spirit" (2 Kings 2:9, NIV). Elijah replied that this was not his to grant. It was God's gift. As we shall see, God gave Elisha all he asked for. God always equips his people to do the things he calls them to do. We, too, can count upon him for the same enabling when our turn comes.

∽

A PRAYER FOR A LISTENING HEART

> *When storms assail and fears prevail,*
> *when fear grips my mind,*

when I'm lonely, lost, and helpless,
and friends are hard to find,
when I'm confused and desperate,
I face a simple choice:
to listen to the devil
or to God's redeeming voice.

He'll whisper grace, I'll see his face;
he'll speak peace to my heart,
when doubt has wrought confusion
and I don't know how to start
to trust again in God's great love
or the power of my King;
then I'll listen to the still small voice
and hear the angels sing.

Lord, meet me now as low I bow
before your great might.
Lord, touch my soul and make me whole
and nerve my heart to fight.
I'll stand upon this mountain
until all my strivings cease,
and through the noise of war I'll hear
your still small voice of peace.
Amen.

Discussion or Journal

1. Review 1 Kings 19:8–21.
2. Why was Horeb referred to as the mountain of God?
3. Why is it helpful to go back to your spiritual roots when you are in trouble?
4. What was Elijah frightened about, and how did God deal with his fears?

5. Share a time you have been in a cave and God has spoken to you in his still small voice. What did he say, and how did you know it was God's voice?
6. Make a list of the ways you can check if the voice you hear is God's voice or Satan's.
7. What should we do when choosing leaders?
8. What can you learn from Elijah about being a mentor? What can you learn from Elisha about being a learner?

Time to Pray
1. Find a "mountain" and stand there in the presence of the Lord.
2. Listen for God's still small voice.
3. Check out the voice you hear to determine if it is God's voice or Satan's.
4. Respond to what the Lord is saying to you. Write your response in your prayer journal.
5. Pray for a mentor or to be one.

To Do on Your Own
1. Read 2 Kings 6:1–7. What is significant about Elisha's response in verse 3?
2. Recall when someone has trained you to take more responsibility in ministry. How did that work?
3. Think over your own ministry. Who might be an Elisha for you?

Notes and Ideas

CHAPTER ELEVEN

LOSING YOUR CUTTING EDGE

———— ❧ ————

AFTER ELIJAH WENT TO HEAVEN IN A FIERY CHARIOT (what other way would you expect him to go?), Elisha began his ministry. His work for God resembles his teacher's in so many ways. There are two incidents in his life that I would like to tell because there are parables in these true stories we can use to teach us about different aspects of prayer. The first is found in 2 Kings 6:1–6, and it has many good applications for our prayer life.

> One day the group of prophets came to Elisha and told him, "As you can see, this place where we meet with you is too small. Let's go down to the Jordan River, where there are plenty of logs. There we can build a new place for us to meet."
>
> "All right," he told them, "go ahead."
>
> "Please come with us," someone suggested.
>
> "I will," he said.
>
> When they arrived at the Jordan, they began cutting down trees. But as one of them was chopping, his ax head fell into the river. "Ah, my lord!" he cried. "It was a borrowed ax!"
>
> "Where did it fall?" the man of God asked. When he showed him the place, Elisha cut a stick and threw it into the water. Then the ax head rose to the surface and floated (2 Kings 6:1–6).

The story shows us the conditions in the schools of the prophets. These had been set up in Israel in Elijah's day, but they had been disbanded under Jezebel's reign of terror. However, they appeared to be thriving. Elisha had been firmly established as head of this work. At this point in the story, he seemed to be living with the students.

Some of the young men living in a community located near the Jordan, a known center of prophetic instruction, came to Elisha and said, "Look, the place where we meet with you is too small for us. Let us go to the Jordan, where each of us can get a pole; and let us build a place there for us to live" (2 Kings 6:1–2, NIV). This was a nice problem to have. The demand for more space for more students is a dilemma many Christian institutions would appreciate having today!

At first Elisha said, "Go," to which one young man replied, "Won't you please come with your servants?" (vv. 2–3). Elisha acquiesced, and so they all went down to the Jordan and, choosing a site, got to work.

Who were these men? They were committed to the work of the Lord, so much so that they had left their homes and brought their families to live in community for a period in order to prepare themselves for effective service. These people were ready to do whatever it took to be highly effective servants of the Lord. As they went to work, one of the young men, using a borrowed ax, wielded it with a little too much enthusiasm, and the ax head fell off into the water. An ax head was a prized and valuable piece of equipment in those days, and the young man was understandably upset. Apparently Elisha was working within earshot, and immediately the man cried out to him, "Oh, my lord,... it was borrowed!" (v. 5).

Elisha asked him, "Where did it fall?" (v. 6). After the young man had shown him the place the ax had fallen in the water, the prophet cut a stick and threw it in there. Then an amazing thing happened. The lost ax head floated to the top of the water, and Elisha told the young man to "lift it out". The relieved servant of the Lord "reached out his hand and took it" (v. 7). Now this is a delightful little miracle that can give us some insight into why we lose effectiveness in our Christian lives.

First of all, we have the man in training. He, like his master Elisha, had burned whatever bridges needed to be burned behind him in order to be in this school. His priorities were in order. There was nothing wrong with his heart. His willingness to put his shoulder to the work was not in dispute. He was in the work contingent that volunteered to do the "donkey work". It mustn't have been an easy task to cut down the huge trees that would be needed to build a large building. No chain saws in those days! So here we have youth married to obvious enthusiasm and total commitment, carrying out the work of the Lord, when all of a sudden he loses his cutting edge! He loses his effectiveness. Right in the middle of serving too.

This can happen to us as well. We can have our Christian life in good order and be in the midst of work at church or in mission and suddenly become aware that something is missing! Things aren't working as they should be. Prayer is boring, the Bible bland, and worship stale. Worse, even though we go through the motions and witness to unbelievers as we get the chance, they don't seem to listen to us the way they used to. In fact, they get the advantage and tie us up in knots in an argument. We have lost our effectiveness.

It is the work of the Holy Spirit to alert us to this. He has an integral part to play in our prayer life. He is the one who will tell us loud and clear when we lose that edge. Witnessing can be likened to cutting down trees in the forest. If we lose our cutting edge and just go on hitting the trees with the handle, we will only hurt the trees. So what does this ax head speak of in my life with Christ?

It speaks of sensitivity to the Spirit's prompting through prayer. What does this mean? Well, it is the Spirit's work to point out when sin enters our lives. As we are on our knees reviewing the day, God through his Spirit will make us aware of a recent conversation or a careless remark we made that hurt someone's feelings. He will do this however he pleases, but one of the ways he alerts us to the fact that our ax head has plopped into the water is by making us aware that we have suddenly become ineffective.

For example, I am speaking at a meeting that has been going quite well. People seem to like me, like what I am saying to them, and appear responsive. Some are actually wiping tears away as I talk! It feels good to be getting this response. I realize I am enjoying myself, but I rationalize this at once and give it a spiritual name. This must be joy, I say to myself. I am just enjoying the gift that God has given me.

But this is not true. Somewhere I have crossed the line between truly enjoying what God has gifted me to do and pride in my part of doing it. The Holy Spirit recognizes this immediately and knows the ax head has just flown off the ax handle! I, however, am not aware anything has occurred. But I can be the last to be aware of it. The Holy Spirit knows it, the people in the audience know it, because they cease to receive anything from me, and eventually I become aware that something is wrong and that somewhere along the line I lost it. I had it, I muse, but I lost it, and that is obvious. I am not talking about losing the Spirit, as I do not believe you can do that once you are born again. I am talking about that flow of the Spirit through us when there is no known, unconfessed sin in our lives. This particular experience is not uncommon among speakers. What happens to me is something that happens to the best of us.

G. Campbell Morgan, a great Bible teacher, was reputed to have said on one occasion that in the middle of a tried-and-true sermon he was preaching, he distinctly heard the "still small voice" whisper in his ear: "Preach on, great preacher, without me!" He had begun to rely on his sermon and not on the Lord, and he lost his effectiveness.

As truly as we learn to recognize our loss, we can learn how to retrieve our "edge" again. It is that cutting edge that is going to make a difference in the projects we are attempting for the Lord. The Holy Spirit wants us to pick up our usefulness again, almost as soon as we lose it. Let me address the part that prayer plays in this renewed usefulness.

ARE YOU HEARING THE HOLY SPIRIT?

An attitude of prayer keeps us in the Holy Spirit's orbit and sensitive to his feelings, so the first thing to do as soon as the Spirit starts to whisper in our ear is to tune in to his "frequency". Open your inner ear to the one who is holy and whose business it is to convict us of sin in all its shapes and forms. Consider the possibility that you are out of line. It could be pride or some other thing that rears its ugly head. It could be that you make a false statement and don't bother to correct it. It may be that you have stopped praying all the time you are talking (it can be done, you know). As soon as you stop depending on the Lord and start depending on yourself, you will notice a subtle but dramatic difference.

Amazingly, you can talk to God at the same time you are talking to your husband, your boss, your friends, or a group of people! As soon as you become aware that this loss has occurred, don't try to analyze it or even stop what you are doing, but call out to your Teacher as the young man cried out to Elisha. A simple cry of help will do. Have you lost your connectedness with God? Do you find yourself at this point of your life flailing away at the trees? Don't go on; cry out for help.

It is no good being dissolute about it either. There appears to be a lot of feeling in the discovery. "Oh, my lord," the man cries. He cares, he really cares. Over and over again I am reminded that God is listening for that "Oh" from us — the expression of heartfelt concern — before he answers us. If you don't have it, pray for it. Ask the Lord to make you care, to really care.

WHERE DID YOU LOSE YOUR EFFECTIVENESS?

What happened to the man in the story when he admitted losing the ax head? Elisha immediately asked him a question. "Where did it fall? Show me the place." God will always ask us where we lost our sharpness. He will want us to be very specific, just as Elisha was with the young man. "Show me the place," he insisted. And we will need to show God the place.

The River of Relationships

I was trying to help a young woman who had, as she put it, lost her peace. "Well," I said, "where exactly did you lose it?" "Exactly?" she echoed. "Exactly," I replied. "Oh, I think it was last year," she tried next. "I didn't ask you *when*, but *where*," I pursued. "Well, I don't want to get into the details," she told me. "I just want God to use me again." "Show me the place," I insisted. Then she told me. "I had had a good ministry with high school students until I moved in with my boyfriend," she admitted. "That will do it," I responded gently. "No wonder you lost your cutting edge." As soon as she showed me the place, I could help her. Helping people recover their usefulness to God is something I delight to do. The first thing is to ask them to show you the place.

There have been many "Jordan Rivers" described to me in my lifetime. There have been many lost ax heads at the bottom of the rivers of wrongdoing. There is the river of wrong relationships, for example. You can even be a missionary and lose your sharp edge on this riverbank. Amy Carmichael fell in love with another missionary, and to outsiders the match seemed perfect. But both felt they could not abandon their work on different continents. During this time, Amy said she was out of sorts and couldn't put a finger on the reason until she realized that this was a wrong relationship, and so the engagement was called off. It's hard when you seem to have two "right people", and yet there's something out of kilter. There was nothing wrong going on in the relationship; it was just that God had something "different" in mind for both Amy and the young man. As soon as she spent a lot of time praying about the problem, the Holy Spirit showed her "the place". They dealt with it and felt better at once!

The Sea of Singleness

Some of us can lose our effectiveness in a Sea of Singleness. This place also had to do with our relationships. Many people are single — some because they chose singleness — but many more are single because singleness chose them!

When I was led to Christ in the hospital, I was asked not to commit my life to Christ unless I was willing to do three things: Remain unmarried; be a missionary; and obey the Lord fully. I was amazed at these options, especially the first one! "Why would I need to be willing to stay single?" I inquired. It was explained to me that there were not too many Christian men in the churches, so there wouldn't be much chance of my getting married. When I inquired why

I couldn't marry a non-Christian, it was explained to me that the Bible spoke very directly to this issue, saying that we were not to marry unbelievers (2 Cor. 6:14). If I was willing to be obedient (the third point), then by the law of averages it would appear that I would not find a man to marry who loved the Lord!

This question set me back on my heels, but as best as I knew how I came to Christ, promising him I would be obedient in the area of my relationships. This initial understanding of the life of obedience saved me from losing my ax head many times in the Sea of Singleness. This did not mean I stopped being a perfectly normal woman who would love to have been married; it just saved me from being discontented in my singleness. I believe we can be contented in the Sea of Singleness if it is God's will for us. Yes, we can even be contented when we are lonely, if we are being obedient to God's call to be single or married.

I meet too many people who are saying publicly that they are willing to be single, yet who are secretly planning to marry! The problem is that there are no secrets that can be kept from the searching eyes of God's Spirit, and there are no inner complaints that he does not hear. Even if you do a pretty good job of keeping your murmurings from everyone else, you will not keep them from him. If you are wondering where you lost your sharpness, perhaps you should look in the Sea of Singleness.

The Lagoon of Loneliness

You might lose your cutting edge in the Lagoon of Loneliness. This does not necessarily relate to the last subject. You can be lonely in a family or even when you are married. You can feel all alone in a crowd of people. You may be ill and in the hospital and, though you are surrounded by people day and night, feel desperately alone. Loneliness is an internal state, not an external one. We can be so obsessed with our lonely feelings that we are distracted from doing God's will and work. Sometimes God asks us to be effective for him even while we are lonely.

The Lake of Laziness

If you do not lose things in the Lagoon of Loneliness, what about the Lake of Laziness? Habits have a habit of slipping. Disciplines get onerous. We feel that we've done our bit and it's someone else's turn, and we complain about it. Or we just succumb to laziness.

At one point in my life, I started to rely on a few good sermons. These were talks that had worked in different places and seemed good to use when I was asked to speak. But I noticed they didn't work all the time. People didn't respond as they used to, and I had a sense of unease. I lost my joy in serving Jesus, and everything got somewhat stale. I cried to the Lord, and the Lord showed me "the place". Once I got around to asking him, he was quick to draw my attention to the problem, and we got it sorted out.

The Bay of Busyness

In contrast to the Lake of Laziness, there is the Bay of Busyness. We cannot be effective on our feet unless we have first been effective on our knees.

There is such a staggering amount of work to be done. But we should think about people more than we think about tasks. Jesus always had time for people, no matter what tasks demanded his attention. One day when he wanted to get away on his own after some bad news, he was interrupted by a multitude of needs in the shape of five thousand hungry people. He put his own needs on hold in order to attend to the needs of others. Jesus fed the crowds and then went away quietly and met with his Father (Matt. 14:23).

Life is necessarily busy, but we must put people before tasks. And we must doggedly spend time with our Father one way or another before our busy day is through. Otherwise, we will lose our edge, and even our time spent with people will not be as effective. I like the little saying above a busy person's desk that reads:

> *Slow me down, Lord, I'm going too fast,*
> *I can't see my brother when he's walking past.*

What's funny is that the key to being productively busy is to be determinedly still. People matter more than things, but God matters more than everything!

The secret is to be still within even when you are busy without, like a needle in a sewing machine. When you watch a sewing machine going full speed, you can hardly see the needle. Yet the needle is resting in the arm, and the arm is powered when the machine is plugged in and turned on. Similarly, when we are plugged in and switched on, when the current of the Holy Spirit is flowing through us, and when we rest in the arm of the Lord, we will be productively busy.

The Pond of Pleasure

There are so many places to lose our ax head, it can get quite hazardous out there! Next, there is the Pond of Pleasure. God wants us to be happy, though not, of course, at the expense of being holy. Joy and happiness are quite different things. My husband has a saying that "happiness depends upon our happenings, and if our happenings don't happen to happen the way we want our happenings to happen, we'll be sad!" Joy, on the other hand, "happens when our happenings don't happen to happen the way we want them to happen." For joy is Jesus who makes our hearts smile. Joy is a Jesus whose presence is experienced in prayer.

The Waters of Worry

The place where I most readily lose my ax head is in the Waters of Worry. As I have said, I seem to have been born a worrier. I am learning to start to pray as soon as I catch myself beginning to get anxious. This works better than anything and gives God a chance to head off the anxiety as soon as it starts. If we don't shape our worries into prayers, our worries will shape us into messed-up people who have nothing to say to a world that is asking for help not to worry! The Bible says, "Be anxious for nothing, but in everything by prayer and supplication, with thanksgiving, let your requests be made known to God; and the peace of God, which surpasses all understanding, will guard your hearts and minds through Christ Jesus" (Phil. 4:6–7, NKJV).

So just where have you lost your effectiveness? Why don't you stop right now and show him the place?

HOW CAN YOU GET SHARP AGAIN?

As soon as the man who had lost the ax head admitted the fact to Elisha and pointed out the exact spot he lost it, Elisha did a strange thing. He threw a stick in the water. He applied a piece of wood to the problem. There is another lesson here.

Confess Anything That Grieves the Spirit

As we confess our sin to God, he will apply the benefits of Christ's death on our behalf. He will apply the wood, that is, the cross on which Christ gave his life for us. The Cross has an application for us every day of our lives. Because Christ died for whatever it is I am confessing, he can forgive and cleanse me on an ongoing basis. He can give me clean hands and a pure heart — a heart that loves him and wants to make a difference.

The Spirit helps us to pray all the right prayers, the prayers that say "Christ is everything", while the devil works to get us to say, "Anything but Christ!" God's Spirit through God's Word will show us the place where we lost the will to want his will, and then we must be obedient to the things he shows us. As we practice the will of God on a daily basis, it should become almost second nature to know when things are not the way they ought to be.

As we come to love God more and more, we will want to grieve him less and less. *Grieve* is a love word. You can't grieve one who doesn't love you. As we spend more and more time with the Lord, we will acquire a knowledge that cannot be learned any other way. We will become sensitive to the things that bring him pleasure and the things that bring him grief. Paul says, "Do not grieve the Holy Spirit of God" (Eph. 4:30, NIV).

It's like being married. When I first got married, I didn't know what brought my husband joy and what brought him grief. I thought I knew, but I really didn't. Now, after forty-two years of marriage, I know instinctively. To the extent that I have taken the trouble to get to know my husband, I have grown to know what makes him happy and, conversely, what upsets him.

Likewise, the longer I "live with God", the more instinctively I know what brings him pleasure. I cannot emphasize enough that there is no shortcut to living effectively for God. Prayer that doesn't work, doesn't work. But even though it is work, it doesn't feel like work at all, because it is love work. For those who do it, it is all joy!

What does the Scripture specifically say about the things that grieve the Spirit? Ruth Paxson, in her book *Life on the Highest Plane*, says it well:

To grieve the Holy Spirit means that we are causing pain to someone who loves us. What, then, in us causes the divine One grief?

He is the Spirit of truth (John 14:17) so anything false, deceitful, hypocritical, grieves him.

He is the Spirit of faith (2 Cor. 4:13) so doubt, unbelief, distrust, worry, anxiety, grieve him.

He is the Spirit of grace (Heb. 10:29) so that which is hard, bitter, ungracious, unthankful, malicious, unforgiving or unloving grieves him.

He is the Spirit of holiness (Rom. 1:4) so anything unclean, defiling or degrading, grieves him.

He is the Spirit of wisdom and revelation (Eph. 1:17) so ignorance, conceit, arrogance and folly grieve him.

He is the Spirit of power, love and self-discipline (2 Tim. 1:7) so that which is barren, fruitless, disorderly, confused and uncontrolled grieves him.

He is the Spirit of life (Rom. 8:2) so anything that savors of indifference, lukewarmness, spiritual dullness, and deadness grieves him.

He is the Spirit of glory (1 Pet. 4:14) so anything worldly, earthly or fleshly grieves him.

As long as we are indulging known sin we are living in the same abode with a grieved Spirit who is thereby hindered from manifesting himself fully in and through us (22–23).

It is a helpful exercise to take a good look at this list on your knees and show the Lord "the place" you lost your ax head. For example, he is the Spirit of faith, and therefore I sometimes grieve him with my worry and anxiety. What do you do that is at odds with who God is?

What happened when Elisha heard the young man's

confession? He applied the wood, and the miracle happened. The iron floated. Through Elisha, God brought the cutting edge back within reach. He can offer us that opportunity by making the iron float. When the Lord sees our contrite hearts, he will make sure we know how to get back on track. He will bring the edge back within reach, but we must put out our hand and take it to ourselves. But maybe you just don't know how to start.

Pray in the Spirit

The Spirit of grace works on so many fronts. When we don't know how to pray, he shows us (Rom. 8:26–27). *The Message* renders the verses: "If we don't know how or what to pray, it doesn't matter. He does our praying in and for us, making prayers out of our wordless sighs, our aching groans. He knows us far better than we know ourselves,... and keeps us present before God."

Many times I have been at a complete loss as to know how or what to pray. After my mother died, I was at a total loss for words. Kneeling down at the side of her coffin, all I could do was offer a deep, wordless sigh. I was immediately conscious that the Spirit took my aching groans and formed them into a prayer for me. I was comforted by the thought that his prayers always get answered too! We are to "build [ourselves] up in [our] most holy faith and pray in the Holy Spirit" (Jude 1:20, NIV).

Praying "in the Holy Spirit" encompasses prayers spoken by you and prayers spoken by the Spirit. When you can pray, do; and when you can't, let him pray for you. If you want to know more about this, ask him to help you to find out. Otherwise, you are not taking advantage of all the avenues of prayer available to you, and your life will be a little blunted. When your life is blunted, however hard you work for the Lord, you will only "hurt the trees".

We read in Romans 8:27 that, "he who searches our hearts knows the mind of the Spirit, because the Spirit intercedes for the saints in accordance with God's will" (NIV). What a comfort to know that the Spirit understands what God wants to do in my life and in the lives of the people I am praying for. If I am in step with the Spirit, he will let me in on his secrets while I am actually praying for them.

Never allow your praying to be stopped because you are distressed about not knowing how to pray. Some of the most effective prayer work is done in our distress, because the Spirit helps our prayers. You can always pray, "Oh, God, you know what you want to do in this hopeless mess. I am at a loss to say a single thing. Pray in me, Lord. Use me to pray the prayers you want prayed in these circumstances, in your name, and for your sake. Amen."

◆

A Prayer to Recover Our Cutting Edge

Dear Savior,
Sharpen my focus,
quicken my lethargic spirit.
Show me where you need to grow me
into a compliant child.
Give me an increasing awareness
of the places where I lose my spiritual edge.
And when I grieve your heart,
may I grow weary with weeping.
Cause my shamefaced soul the consternation it should know
when I resist your promptings.
Mend me, as you mind me, that you and I may be as one,
united in purpose as you bring a lost world to its senses.
Ready me for battle as you win my wars.

Steady me for conflict in the inner halls of your residence.
Teach me abandonment to your love and service.
Look upon me, and love me into your likeness —
before you bring me home!
I love you, Lord.
Amen.

Discussion or Journal

1. Think of other biblical examples of people who lost their "cutting edge".
2. Where did they lose it?
   a. the River of Relationships
   b. the Sea of Singleness
   c. the Lagoon of Loneliness
   d. the Lake of Laziness
   e. the Bay of Busyness
   f. the Pond of Pleasure
   g. the Waters of Worry
3. Where have you lost your cutting edge?
4. Review the steps to recovery:
   a. Confess how you have grieved the Holy Spirit.
   b. Pray in the Spirit — with his help.
5. Review Rom. 8:26–27. What part does the Holy Spirit play in prayer? Are there any examples in your own life?

Time to Pray

1. If we are serious about keeping our cutting edge, then we will need to pray about it. Spend time asking God to show you the place in which you lost your effectiveness. Realize that you live by grace on borrowed time with borrowed gifts and borrowed opportunities. You can say, along with the young prophet in training, "Oh, my Lord, it was borrowed." Ask him to forgive you and cleanse you.

2. Pray for people who have lost their sharpness.
3. Pray that those who haven't lost their edge will keep it.
4. Pray for more people to learn how to pray in the Spirit.

To Do on Your Own
1. Read 2 Kings 6:8–17, and write out the story in your own words with your observations.
2. Practice being aware of your cutting edge.
3. Pray in the Spirit according to Romans 8:26–27.

Notes and Ideas

CHAPTER TWELVE

CHARIOTS OF FIRE

IN THE LAST CHAPTER WE LIKENED OUR PRAYER LIFE TO an ax head. We talked about how important it is to stay sharp and how ineffective we are if we lose our edge. Keeping our "edge" is so important because we are living in a war zone. There is a battle raging around us that most people are quite unaware of. Unseen forces that wish to trap us in impossible situations surround us. But "if God is for us, who can be against us?" (Rom. 8:31, NIV). The battle is the Lord's, and we know the end of the story!

The last chapter in this book is challenging to write. There are so many good books that deal with spiritual warfare and that cover so much material on that topic. I want to look at a small incident in the life of Elisha and see how one man's particular spiritual battle was resolved. There are lots of good parallels here for us to learn from. The story is found in 2 Kings 6 and follows the incident of the lost ax head.

When the king of Aram was at war with Israel, he would confer with his officers and say, "We will mobilize our forces at such and such a place."

But immediately Elisha, the man of God, would warn the king of Israel, "Do not go near that place, for the Arameans are planning to mobilize their troops there." So the king of Israel would send word to the place indicated by the man of God, warning the people there to be on their guard. This happened several times.

The king of Aram became very upset over this. He called in his officers and demanded, "Which of you is the traitor? Who has been informing the king of Israel of my plans?"

"It's not us, my lord," one of the officers replied. "Elisha, the prophet in Israel, tells the king of Israel even the words you speak in the privacy of your bedroom!"

The king commanded, "Go and find out where Elisha is, and we will send troops to seize him."

And the report came back: "Elisha is at Dothan" (2 Kings 6:8–13).

At this point, Elisha is on good terms with the king of Israel, King Jehoram. He has been advising him on what to do with a dangerous political situation. We know that the king respected Elisha because he addresses him as "my father" (2 Kings 6:21). He had good reason to respect the prophet because Elisha had been warning him not to take the army to certain places because the Arameans were lying in wait for them. Israel and the Arameans had returned to intermittent warfare. But time after time Elisha miraculously knew what was going to happen and warned the king of Israel.

The king of the Arameans grew furious and accused his own leaders of treachery. "Will you not tell me which of us is on the side of the king of Israel?" he demanded. Whereupon one of his officers answered, "None of us, my lord the king,… but Elisha, the prophet who is in Israel, tells the king of Israel the very words you speak in your bedroom" (2 Kings 6:11–12, NIV).

At this, the angry Aramean king sent a strong force to capture Elisha and bring him back to him. Having discovered that Elisha was at Dothan, the king sent the horses and chariots at night, and the soldiers took up their positions during darkness. They completely surrounded the city, but unknown to them, there was another army there already! It was the Lord's army. This army was just as real and a lot more powerful than any earthly army, for it was under the command of the Lord of hosts himself.

Elisha's servant got up early in the morning and went outside. I like to think that, being under the influence of a man like Elisha, this servant had learned that early morning was an excellent time to meet with the Lord. And I can see him fastening back the shutters and settling down for his devotions, when he looked around and got a very nasty shock. The enemy surrounded them! Well, that was enough to stop his devotions in a hurry, and he raced into the house to blurt out the bad news to Elisha.

So one night the king of Aram sent a great army with many chariots and horses to surround the city. When the servant of the man of God got up early the next morning and went outside, there were troops, horses, and chariots everywhere.

"Ah, my lord, what will we do now?" he cried out to Elisha.

"Don't be afraid!" Elisha told him. "For there are more on our side than on theirs!" Then Elisha prayed, "O Lord, open his eyes and let him see!" The Lord opened his servant's eyes, and when he looked up, he saw that the hillside around Elisha was filled with horses and chariots of fire.

As the Aramean army advanced toward them, Elisha prayed, "O Lord, please make them blind." And the Lord did as Elisha asked. Then Elisha went out and told them, "You have come the wrong way! This isn't the right city! Follow me, and I will take you to the man you are looking for." And he led them to Samaria. As soon as they had entered Samaria, Elisha prayed, "O Lord, now open their eyes and let them see." And the Lord did, and they discovered that they were in Samaria.

When the king of Israel saw them, he shouted to Elisha, "My father, should I kill them?"

"Of course not!" Elisha told him. "Do we kill prisoners of war? Give them food and drink and send them home again to their master."

So the king made a great feast for them and then sent them home to their king. After that, the Aramean raiders stayed away from the land of Israel (2 Kings 6:14–23).

Elisha, of course, knew all about it already, as he and God had been discussing what to do about the situation. Elisha would want to know what God had in mind in the greater scheme of things. Apparently God wanted to give the people of Israel one more opportunity to repent and get their act together, and so he had a plan of deliverance in mind.

The servant was terrified, but Elisha reassured him and prayed that God would open his eyes. "O Lord, open his eyes so he may see" (2 Kings 6:17, NIV). It was a short prayer but to the point! It was all there was time for perhaps, or maybe it came at the end of a long season of prayer that Elisha had been having about the situation. At this point, Elisha could see the army of the Lord, but perhaps he had needed reassurance himself that God was firmly in control. His short prayer for the same reassurance for his servant was all that was necessary, and God answered it! And when God answered Elisha's prayer for a heavenly vision, the man stopped being afraid. Surrounding them were horses and chariots the likes of which he had never seen. They covered the hills that surrounded the city. These were fantastic chariots of fire that made the iron ones the Arameans were sitting in look a bit silly! Then Elisha said to his servant: "Don't be afraid.... Those who are with us are more than those who are with them" (2 Kings 6:16, NIV).

Then God worked a miracle and struck the entire Aramean army with blindness, and Elisha led them off to Samaria straight into the hands of the king of Israel! (2 Kings 6:18–20). The king of Israel was beside himself at his good fortune and excitedly asked Elisha if he should slaughter all the soldiers. But the prophet restrained him and told him that that wasn't the way to treat prisoners of war and that they should prepare a sumptuous feast for them instead and send them on their way (2 Kings 6:21–22). This gracious treatment overwhelmed the soldiers and subsequently kept them off Israel's back for a good long while: "So the bands from Aram stopped raiding Israel's territory" (2 Kings 6:23, NIV).

What a wonderful story, and what prayer lessons it contains. Who is in control here? God is. He is firmly in the saddle, or rather, the chariot! His Captain of the hosts of heaven is on the scene overseeing operations. So take courage, those of you who have just woken up to a new day and have found yourselves surrounded by unexpected danger in whatever form it takes.

SOMEONE WANTS US DESTROYED

Spiritual danger does take many forms, but the forces behind it all have one goal in mind: our destruction. Paul tells us to be aware of this and "be self-controlled and alert. Your enemy the devil prowls around like a roaring lion looking for someone to devour" (1 Pet. 5:8, NIV). There is a devil, and he has lots of help. The Bible tells us his name is Satan and that he once occupied a prominent position in heaven. One eternal day he decided he didn't want to worship God anymore. He wanted God to worship him, so there was war in heaven, and he was thrown out. Jesus told his disciples, "I saw Satan fall like lightning from heaven" (Luke 10:18, NIV). Many angels joined him in his rebellion, and since he was thrown out into the earth, we still have to contend with him trying to get us to worship him instead of God. He even tried to get the Lord Jesus to do that! When Satan tempted Jesus in the wilderness, he took him to a very high mountain and showed him all the kingdoms of the world and their splendor. "'All this I will give you,' he said, 'if you will bow down and worship me'" (Matt. 4:9, NIV).

Satan will do everything to try to keep people from coming to Christ. He doesn't want people to have their eyes opened to spiritual realities, and so he blinds them. "The god of this age has blinded the minds of unbelievers, so that they cannot see the light of the gospel of the glory of Christ, who is the image of God" (2 Cor. 4:4, NIV). Once he loses that battle and someone comes to faith, he will do everything to hinder the effectiveness of a Christian who is growing in the faith.

And so he uses all means at his disposal, as "prince of the power of the air" to achieve his objectives. He may use outright physical abuse, as in war or killing. Jesus told us that Satan "was a murderer from the beginning" (John 8:44). Or he may play mind games with us. You can't stop Satan whispering in your ears, but you can resist him and "he will flee from you" (James 4:7). Like the army that surrounded Elisha, the devil's forces surround us, but God is here too. He threw Satan out of heaven, and he can throw him out of our minds. In the end, Satan is only a created being, a created being that went bad, very bad, while God is the Creator of all things; he is uncreated, self-sustaining, and all powerful.

SATAN IS STILL AT WORK TODAY

Satan used the Arameans to do his work in Elisha's day, and he uses armies today. Think of the rise of Hitler and all the world wars there have been. But the devil also uses other more subtle means to trap and destroy us.

A middle-aged lady confided in me that she had been on the Internet and had inadvertently come across a chat room that looked interesting. So she started visiting it and got involved in a relationship that fed her need for companionship. She had a bad marriage, and it soon got a lot worse as she became enmeshed in a relationship she had no business having. She knew it was wrong but couldn't bear the thought of doing without it. We talked for a long time. She had a miserable face because she was doing a miserable thing!

I asked her if she would like to be free from it. She looked tormented, and I felt really bad for her. "Oh, yes," she replied in answer to my question. "But it's too strong for me. I feel helpless in the face of the forces pulling me in this direction." I told her about the chariots of fire surrounding her. She didn't "see" them. I talked till I was blue in the face, but she was so fearful to let go of this relationship, and she felt that these evil forces were jut too strong for her. So I invited her to talk with the Captain of the Lord's hosts with me. I asked her if I could pray for her. "Yes, please do," she responded looking scared.

So we stood together, and I took her hand and prayed an "Elisha" prayer. "Oh, Lord, open her eyes." I prayed that she would see what the servant saw. I prayed that she would see the space around her alive with the angels of God. I prayed that she would realize "that those that were with her were more than those that were with them". I prayed she would see what I saw and what countless other ordinary servants of the Lord have seen down through the ages. And then I said amen, and I gave her a hug and went my way.

I saw her the next day. She didn't look that different, but there was something there that hadn't been there before — a hope, a whisper of relief and expectation. "Perhaps God is strong enough to help me break it off," she whispered to me, and then added, "if he's not too mad with me!" "The enemy is vastly outnumbered," I reminded her. "I know, I know," she said smiling (for the first time!). "You and your chariots of fire! I only hope you are right."

People desperately want us to be right about those chariots of fire. They are surrounded by the enemy, an enemy that would have no compunction in capturing them and taking them shackled "home" to their king. But the Captain of our salvation, the Lord of hosts, takes a dim view of this. He loves all of us. He loves you, and he loves me, and he loves that lady struggling with the Arameans. He died for her. He does not appreciate the fact that these evil beings laid in wait for her, ambushed her, and she succumbed. But on his cross our Savior made a fool of these evil powers. Paul, writing to the Christians at Colosse, said, "Having disarmed the powers and authorities, [Christ] made a public spectacle of them, triumphing over them by the cross" (Col. 2:15, NIV). He won the victory then, so we could win the victory now. We must pray for this woman and all the other women in our world who don't know about the chariots of fire!

What an experience this must have been for the servant of Elisha. We don't know his name. Whoever he was, he experienced one of the most exciting things that a son of the prophets could experience. He saw the Host of heaven with his own eyes! And this happened in answer to another's prayer on his behalf. When we get around to prayer warfare, we need to start by praying for the servants of Elisha. We can pray as Elisha prayed: "Oh, Lord, open their eyes to heavenly realities. Let them see that you are firmly in control of this situation, however frightening it may appear to be. And deliver them, Lord, from their fears."

GOD WILL LET US GLIMPSE HIS HEAVENLY FORCES

I am not suggesting that God will prove his presence in just the same way he proved it to Elisha and his servant. But, as he wills, he will answer our prayer for a glimpse of spiritual reality. We human beings don't usually have such visions — in fact some of us never have anything like this happen to us in a lifetime. But now and again, God gives those of us who pray, or those we pray for, a glimpse of the forces of heaven employed on our behalf. These assurances often come in the most ordinary ways, but at just the right times!

It may be like the woman struggling with her Internet relationship that God uses a speaker at a conference. Or as we are reading the Bible we "see" through a verse of Scripture the horses and chariots of fire that surround us in our troubles. God's Word enlightens us, and God's Spirit applies to our lives the truth that we read. Some Scriptures tell us that God's angels camp round about his people, and these give us hope. Or it may be a psalm or a promise that puts our fears to rest.

Sometimes God uses dreams. When Joseph was un-aware that King Herod was going to slaughter all the little boys under two years of age in the region where he and Mary, the mother of Jesus, were living, an angel warned him in a dream to take his family to safety in Egypt (Matt. 2:13). Joseph obeyed and learned that those who were with him were more than those who were against him.

The eye-opening assurance that "God is for us" can, of course, come to us through Scripture, dreams, visions, books, tapes, preaching, teaching, or any other way God designs. He is not limited. In a rare moment, God may open people's physical eyes to actually see spiritual realities as in the case of

Elisha's servant, and people see what is unseen to others around them. One way or another, God wants to open the eyes of all of us to what we need to see and understand to be our heavenly resources. This will happen in answer to believing prayer.

Paul talked about "the eyes of your heart" (Eph. 1:18, NIV). In fact, he prayed specifically for the Ephesians, that the eyes of their hearts would be opened to hope, spiritual riches, and the power that God makes available to those who believe. Paul went on to talk about the power, authority, and dominion in the heavenly realms, which God has put under the feet of Christ (Eph. 1:21–22). There is a special blessing for those of us who use the eyes of our heart to "see" that "if God is for us, who can possibly be against us?" I find that it is in prayer that a lot of that "seeing" is done. It is at the feet of him who has conquered those hostile unseen powers by his death on the cross that fear is turned into faith. What can this story teach us? What applications can we draw?

Don't Panic When You See the Enemy
The first lesson is not to panic when we see the enemy. The servant was panicked when he first saw the Aramean army, and who can blame him? I would have been panicked too! To be trapped like that with no viable means of escape must have been very frightening. If all of us could see what is going on around us in the unseen world, we probably would all panic and not be able to function. It is the grace of God that shields us from knowing too much about the horrible spiritual forces that work in the darkness of our fallen environment. Maybe those who have experienced war and have found themselves threatened by the enemy have a better idea of what this feels like than we do. I have only once been in such a situation.

Stuart and I were in Colombia, South America, at a

missionary base that was surrounded by guerrillas. We were there for a conference and had reason to believe we were all in some danger. There was no hedge or wall around the property, and one of the men on the base had been kidnapped a short while before. The leaders of the center took great care of us, and we were given code names and given escorts as we moved about the base. Stuart's and my code names were Abraham and Sarah!

I was so glad that we went to minister to the personnel there on that missionary base, and I was so glad that God kept us safe. But as I left at the end of our two short weeks, I had a new appreciation for the many missionaries who live and work in similar difficult situations around the world.

To walk along the path to the meeting room meant walking along the edge of the property next to the jungle. Every shadow seemed menacing, and every noise made me jump. The iron chariots were out there, and we knew it. Every morning as we prayed together, I would pray in the words of the servant of Elisha, "O Lord, what shall we do?" Every morning after our time of prayer, we would know what we had to do, and we would do it. The thing that was vital was to have our spiritual eyes open to the fact that though there were undoubtedly hostile forces out there that intended to do us harm, there were more forces on our side than on theirs!

Cry Out to the Lord

When you are surrounded by the enemy, cry out to the Lord. Since the enemy will always surround you while you live on this earth, prayer — the means of communicating with the one in control — will become a constant necessity. Can I encourage you to cry out and keep on crying out? Acknowledge your helplessness, which is, if you remember, the basis of all effective praying. The more challenges we face, the more opportunities we have to cast "all [our] care upon Him, for He cares for [us]" (1 Pet. 5:7, NKJV). The NLT renders this: "Give all your worries and cares to God, for he cares about what happens to you". Whereas Phillips says, "You can throw the whole weight of your anxieties upon him, for you are his personal concern" (1 Pet. 5:7, Phillips). Having our spiritual eyes open to the fact we are his personal concern should give us a little bit of confidence.

Prayer is time to cast, to throw the weight of our burdens on the Lord of hosts. Just get on your knees, knowing that enemies surround you, even though you don't see them, and throw all your panicky feelings in his direction! Peter reminds his correspondents, "He cares about what happens to you."

So first God wants you dependent. He wants to know you will run into his strong arms because there is nowhere left to run. When people see you do this, then they will know who you belong to. Elisha's servant belonged to Elisha. He literally rushed into the house to his master as soon as he saw the menacing army. It was obvious whom he had confidence in. He knew where to head when he was overwhelmed.

Years ago I was on a train. There is not much to do when you are on a train, so everyone watches everyone else. There was a little girl flitting here and there, talking with all the passengers. None of us could figure out to whom she belonged. Just when you thought you knew, she would climb up on someone else's lap, and you would realize that you'd been wrong! Then the train suddenly disappeared into a long, dark tunnel. The little girl flew straight into her daddy's arms, crying, "Daddy, Daddy!" Now everyone in that railway car knew exactly whom the child belonged to!

For some of us, it takes entering a long dark tunnel for us to throw ourselves into our Father's arms. It takes a sudden and terrible darkness to cause us to cast all our anxieties on him. We noticed that after the train had gone through that tunnel, the little girl stayed close to her father. She didn't flit around so much! That's what long, dark tunnels do to you!

So what is the dark tunnel you are in right now? Is it a tunnel of divorce or a tunnel of disappointment? Is it a sickness or depression that just won't lift? Maybe it is a temptation that has you by the throat. Or is it a fear that just won't go away? I hope you have a relationship with your heavenly Father so that you can throw the weight of all your pain and burden in his direction. One good thing about showing the people on the train to whom you belong is that it gives them ideas! Can you imagine what it is like to be in the long dark tunnel all alone? Well, try to imagine it, because that is what most people experience.

Find a Friend to Help You

Once Elisha's servant was in the house and he had cried out to his master, Elisha said, "Don't be afraid!" (2 Kings 6:16). Well, pigs may fly! How do you "do not the do nots"? It's all fine for someone to tell you to stop being afraid, but what if you try and the fear is still firmly gripping your heart? God would not tell us to not fear if it wasn't possible to obey him. Fear torments, and God does not want his children tormented. But God never gives us a command to obey without the means to obey it. What were the means he made available to Elisha's servant?

First, he put someone in his life who could help him, another servant who could see what he couldn't yet see. He wants us to help each other with these issues of life. Look around you. Find a friend to help you. Look for someone who is just a little way ahead of you in the journey of life, a person who can see spiritual realities a little more clearly than you can. It can be someone who has walked this way before and has lived to tell the tale. It doesn't have to be an Elisha, either; there are not too many spiritual giants around. It might be another servant just like you.

When I was having our first child, I was pretty apprehensive. I was in a large teaching hospital, where things were run very efficiently. The nurses looked far too young for my liking, but I supposed they knew what they were doing. I was assigned a particularly young-looking one, and my fears were confirmed when she told me it was her first year of nursing! Great, I thought. Just my luck. I looked around to see if I could swap with someone else's nurse, but they all looked like they just came out of primary school and, anyway, none of them were married, so what did they know about having children?

A cleaning lady was there, mopping up an already spotless floor. She, being very friendly and seeing my frightened face, said, "Oh, don't worry dearie, I've had ten children! There's nothing to it." I grabbed her hand so hard she winced. "Will you come with me into the delivery room?" I begged her. "Oh, dearie, I couldn't do that," she said. "I'm not a nurse." "But you've been there," I pleaded. "You know!" She had been through the long, dark tunnel of the birth process and lived to tell the tale. I needed her at that moment very badly. They didn't let me take her into the delivery room with me, of course, and my young nurse did okay, but I had heard the word I needed to hear from the one I needed to hear it from, and I set about my work strengthened for the task.

Once You Have Been Helped, Help Others
Once you have been helped, you can be the one who helps another. Whom do you know who is in need of some peace of mind? Someone who is going through chemotherapy,

perhaps? Maybe you have been down that road and you can draw near to this person and say, "Don't be afraid." All you need to do to have a ministry to hurting people is to be one step ahead of them in life experience and in knowledge of God's help in times of trouble. How did God help you through the Scripture? You could jot down the verse that lifted your spirits — write it on a card and post it. How did a hymn lift your mood? Was a book just the encouragement you needed? Did someone come and pray for you? You could return the favor. What was it that opened your eyes to the battle going on around you? You could share this in some way.

Elisha was in far more danger than his servant was. The soldiers didn't want his servant; they wanted him, yet Elisha was not afraid. He had "been there, done that, and got the T-shirt!" Because he was just a little ahead of his servant, he could look back and see how God had been for him a "refuge and strength, a very present help in trouble" (Ps. 46:1, NKJV). He could look ahead and know that God would come to take him home when his time came. Insight like that can change the world. It had changed Elisha's world, and now he was ready to help others.

I love the part of the story where Elisha is given the clue to the enemy's movements and warns his king. I like this part because the Bible tells us to "know our enemy" too. We are not to be ignorant of Satan's devices. The better we know the Word of God, the better we will be able to warn others of his movements and help them avoid him. Elisha had learned to see the unseen, and he was eager to help his servant to do the same. It didn't mean he was so heavenly minded that he was of no earthly use. He wasn't in denial about the evil around them. He just knew that those that were with them were more than those that were against them. He knew the end of the story and could be at peace.

See the Chariots of Fire

So what do we need to "see" in order to know peace of mind when all that is in our face is the enemy? One way or another we need to see chariots of fire! The chariots of fire are all around us. Angels from the realms of glory have come to our realm on the order of the King of kings and Lord of lords. These are legions and legions of angels under the command of a Captain who loved us and died for us. As I have already said, most of us will never see them with our physical eyes, but we can learn to see them with the eyes of true faith, as Elisha and his servant did.

These are the soldiers of the Lord's army that will garrison our hearts and minds with the peace of God. God's peace corps is not operating in a peaceful environment; God's peace corps garrisons our souls in the midst of war, according to Philippians 4:7. As surely as those fiery chariots garrisoned the house of Elisha and his servant, so will God's soldiers of peace "police" our thoughts and refuse to let anyone through to terrorize us!

It helps to count the soldiers. To inventory the chariots. To take note that there are far, far more of them than of our enemies! Do you believe this? The Scripture talks a lot about angels. In Hebrews it says: "[God] makes his angels winds, his servants flames of fire" (Heb. 1:7, NIV). God calls his angels "messengers swift as the wind, and servants made of flaming fire" (Heb. 1:7). And again in Psalm 104:3–4 it says: "He makes the clouds his chariot and rides on the wings of the wind. He makes winds his messengers, flames of fire his servants" (NIV). When Peter drew a sword to protect Jesus in the Garden of Gethsemane, Jesus said that if he (Jesus) wanted rescuing, all he would have to do was to call to his Father, who would "at once put at my disposal more than twelve legions of angels? But how then would the Scriptures be fulfilled?" (Matt. 26:53–54, NIV). God has all the angels he needs to deal with all the puny soldiers on earth. Earth's soldiers are nothing but little "dust men". God's soldiers, on the other hand, are fire men! Do we believe this? Can we "see" this with the eyes of our hearts? If we can, we will have gone a long way toward dealing with our fears.

Praise God for the Outcome

And then we can begin to praise God for all the things that he will show us of the unseen world. As we affirm our belief in the superiority of the Lord, above all powers on earth and in the heavenlies, we can begin to praise him for the sure outcome of the conflict. Praise is a fierce weapon! Praise shoots fear stone dead! Praise starts talking about the end of the story. It triumphs over its foes. It takes control of its enemies as surely as Elijah took control of the blinded army and captured them. Sin or fear will not have dominion over you — God promised!

So what do I do when I look out of the window of my world and am panicked with the things I see going on around me? Where do I turn when I see the opposition up close? To the Lord! He is ahead of the game. He is prepared to show himself strong on our behalf. So if "God is for us, who can be against us?" Prayer opens our eyes to this incredible reality, the reality that God is not absent even when we cannot see him. He will keep us calm in the crisis. He will show us what to do. He always anticipates our dilemmas because he knows everything there is to know, even the words our enemies speak in their bedchamber! This must drive the devil crazy!

The devil and all his forces will, as Charles Wesley put it, "seek to work us woe". Just as Satan instigated the Aramean forces to try to stop Elisha and his servant from having their prayer time, so he will move against any of us who are in tune with the God of heaven and earth, and in tune with his purposes. But God is ahead of Satan, just as he was ahead of the Aramean forces. He is working out his purposes, and his will will prevail, his glory will be revealed, his name will be honored, and his power will be let loose in the world.

What do you think Elisha felt like, leading all those blind soldiers into the hands of the king of Israel? Triumphant, I expect! And so he should. And so should you and I. We should consistently experience victory in our walk with God. It is ironic that God struck the forces of evil blind at the same time he opened his servant's eyes! He answered both of Elisha's prayers. But then Elisha, like his master Elijah before him, knew how to pray prayers that work!

ABOVE ALL, PRAY!

I would not want to finish this book without praying that in some way the words written here will furnish you with weapons — weapons to do battle in the name of the Lord. Above all, I pray that you will pray! Pray as you have never prayed before, and with great effect, as you "fix [your] eyes on Jesus, the author and perfecter of our faith.... Consider him who endured such opposition from sinful men, so that you will not grow weary and lose heart" (Heb. 12:2–3, NIV). Prayer is the "place" you go to fix your gaze. Then, having seen the face of God, do not grow weary and lose heart.

As Paul puts it:

> Therefore, we do not lose heart. Though outwardly we are wasting away, yet inwardly we are being renewed day by day. For our light and momentary troubles are achieving for us an eternal glory that far outweighs them all. So we fix our eyes not on what is seen, but on what is unseen. For what is seen is temporary, but what is unseen is eternal (2 Cor. 4:16–18, NIV).

Hallelujah, amen!

❧

A Prayer from Our Hearts to His

Hay in his hair and stars in his eyes,
cradled in crib, quiet he lies.
What does he know, and who does he see —
needy humanity like you and me?

Dust in his sandals, chisel in hand,
building a fine house in Nazareth land.
What is he thinking; what's on his mind —
is he mourning the family he'll soon leave behind?

Stone for his pillow, a traveling man,
healing and helping, preaching God's plan,
proving his deity, rejected by those
who should have known better than being his foes.

Cross on his shoulder, thorns on his brow,
whipped like a dog and kicked like a cow,
slapped by tormentors, tortured and torn —
dear God, was he sorry he'd ever been born?

Early one morning, long before dawn,
folding the grave clothes he'd worn for his own,
rising to bless us and willing to come
into our poor hearts to call them his home.

Spirits abundant, life from the tomb,
bursting earth's barriers into this room,
we'll live for your pleasure — oh bless with your smile —
may our dedication make Calvary worthwhile.
Amen.

Discussion or Journal

1. Review 2 Kings 6:8–23. What was the reason Elisha gave his servant for not being afraid? (v. 16)
2. Look up the following references, and make a list of the facts you discover about Satan and his work.
   a. Genesis 3:14
   b. Job 1:6
   c. John 12:31
   d. 2 Corinthians 11:4
   e. Hebrews 2:14
   f. Revelation 9:11
   g. Revelation 20:2, 7
3. Write out and memorize 2 Kings 6:16, "Don't be afraid!… For there are more on our side than on theirs!"
4. Discuss what it means to "see" the unseen.
5. How can we pray for those who are falling for the devil's lies?
6. Make a list of those whom the devil has blinded to the truth. What could you do to help them?

Time to Pray

1. Pray for all the teenagers you know who are frightened.
2. Pray for all the adults.
3. Pray a Scripture for them.
4. Pray for all the missionaries who are surrounded by hostility.
5. Pray for all the pastors and their families who are under attack.
6. Pray for your neighbors and friends who are blinded to the truth.
7. Pray for yourself.

Notes and Ideas

ABOUT THE AUTHOR

Jill Briscoe is the author (or co-author with her husband, Stuart, and her daughter, Judy) of more than forty books, including study guides, devotional material, a study Bible, poetry, and children's books. God has used Jill's wisdom, wit, and disarming honesty to touch the hearts of men and women as she speaks around the world, challenging her listeners to surrender their lives to Christ and live in obedience to him.

In addition to her active speaking and writing schedule, Jill serves as advisor to the women's ministries at Elmbrook Church in Brookfield, Wisconsin, where Stuart has served as senior pastor since 1970. She is the executive editor of *Just Between Us*, a magazine published to provide encouragement, inspiration, spiritual support, and practical insights for ministry wives and women in church, parachurch, and missions leadership. She also advises numerous non-profit organizations and serves on the board of directors for World Relief Corporation and Christianity Today, Inc.

Along with Stuart, Jill directs Telling the Truth media ministries, which provide radio and television ministries as well as resources in books and tapes. Jill and Stuart enjoy not only their three grown children (David, Judy, and Peter — all of whom are in ministry) but also their thirteen grandchildren.